FLOWCHARTS

Plain & Simple

Learning and Application Guide

oriel®

Flowcharts: Plain & Simple

Copyright © 2002 Oriel Incorporated. All Rights Reserved.
The contents of this publication may not be reproduced in whole or in any part without written consent of Oriel Incorporated.
3800 Regent St.   P.O. Box 5445   Madison   WI 53705-0445   USA
Ph: (608) 238-8134   FAX: (608) 238-2908   Customer Service: (800) 669-8326

This product represents the combined efforts of many, many talented people. Oriel Incorporated would like to recognize the following people for their contributions:

Lynda Finn	Subject Matter Expert	George Hettich	Reviewer
Casey Garhart	Instructional Designer and Developer	Kevin Little	Reviewer
		Ron Snee	Reviewer
Barbara Streibel	Project Leader	Mary English	Copy Editor
Brian Sullivan	Materials Production	Sue Reynard	Copy Editor
Jennifer Livesey	Materials Production	Chris Foss	Proofreader
Jan Angell	Materials Production	Mara Scanlon	Proofreader
Pat Zander	Marketing	Ken Ezrow	Researcher
Vickie Benchlikha	Production	Mary Hollinger	Administrative Assistant
Dale Mann	Cartoonist		

We also thank all the people who helped us test and improve early drafts of this product.

About Oriel Incorporated
Oriel Incorporated provides consulting and training services, and learning resources designed to help your organization increase its business performance. Our expertise includes six sigma methodologies, lean manufacturing, strategic plan implementation, implementing teams, leadership development, process improvement, process management, data collection and analysis, voice of the customer, and facilitating the combining of cultures and processes for mergers and acquisitions. The Team Handbook Second Edition is just one of the training resources designed to help you build the internal skills and knowledge you need to thrive in today's competittive world.

ISBN 1-884731-03-1

Table of Contents

INTRODUCTION 1

SECTION A: A Brief Guide to Flowcharts 7
    Definition of a Flowchart 8
    Flowchart Symbols 12
    Useful Flowchart Features 14
    When to Use Which Flowchart 33

SECTION B: Detailed Flowcharts 35
    Definition 36
    Construction Techniques 48
    Creating a Detailed Flowchart 50

SECTION C: Opportunity Flowcharts 55
    Definition 56
    Value-Added and Cost-Added-Only 63
    Creating an Opportunity Flowchart 76

SECTION D: Deployment Flowcharts 81
    Definition 82
    Construction Techniques 94
    Creating a Deployment Flowchart 104

HIGHLIGHTS 109

GLOSSARY 113

REFERENCES 117

Flowcharts: Plain & Simple

© 2002 Oriel Incorporated. All Rights Reserved.

Learning and Application Guides

INTRODUCTION TO THE TOOLS: *Plain & Simple*
> Everything you need to know about the basics but are too busy to ask

DATA COLLECTION: *Plain & Simple*
> Everything you need to know about data collection but are too busy to ask

HOW TO GRAPH: *Plain & Simple*
> Everything you need to know about graphing data but are too busy to ask

FLOWCHARTS: *Plain & Simple*
> Everything you need to know about flowcharts but are too busy to ask

PARETO CHARTS: *Plain & Simple*
> Everything you need to know about Pareto charts but are too busy to ask

TIME PLOTS: *Plain & Simple*
> Everything you need to know about time plots but are too busy to ask

INDIVIDUALS CHARTS: *Plain & Simple*
> Everything you need to know about individuals charts but are too busy to ask

FREQUENCY PLOTS: *Plain & Simple*
> Everything you need to know about frequency plots but are too busy to ask

SCATTER PLOTS: *Plain & Simple*
> Everything you need to know about scatter plots but are too busy to ask

CAUSE-AND-EFFECT DIAGRAMS: *Plain & Simple*
> Everything you need to know about cause-and-effect diagrams but are too busy to ask

ORDERING INFORMATION

To order call Oriel Incorporated Sales and Service at 1-800-669-8326, weekdays 8:00 A.M. to 5:00 P.M. (Central time). Outside the United States and Canada call 1-608-238-8134.

Flowcharts: Plain & Simple

© 2002 Oriel Incorporated. All Rights Reserved.

INTRODUCTION

What You Will Learn

This guide covers the types of flowcharts most often used to look at the flow of work in organizations.

The first section provides a brief introduction to the value of flowcharts and an overview of different types of flowcharts and their uses.

The remaining sections show how to create and interpret three specific types of flowcharts: detailed, opportunity, and deployment flowcharts.

Getting the Most Out of This Guide

Flowcharts are basically pictures of processes. Before you begin you should have a basic understanding of what a process is and how processes relate to your own work.

For more information on how this tool fits with others in an improvement context, see *Introduction to the Tools: Plain & Simple*.

For more information on processes and process thinking, see Joiner's *Fundamentals of Fourth Generation Management*.

INTRODUCTION

INTRODUCTION

Flowcharts

Purpose

Flowcharts are tools that help us understand, standardize, and improve our work processes. This guide introduces three kinds of flowcharts. It explains what these flowcharts are, when to use each type, how to interpret them, and how to construct them.

Objectives

Working through this guide will help you become familiar with how to construct and use three kinds of flowcharts. The list below shows what you learn in each section.

Section A: Introduction
- Know what a flowchart is and what it does
- Recognize the types of flowcharts used to improve work processes
- Know the features a good flowchart should have
- Understand how a flowchart can help identify problems in a process

Section B: Detailed Flowcharts
- Know what a detailed flowchart is
- Know when to use a detailed flowchart
- Understand how a detailed flowchart can help identify process problems
- Know the critical components of a detailed flowchart
- Be able to construct a detailed flowchart

Section C: Opportunity Flowcharts
- Know what an opportunity flowchart is
- Know when to use an opportunity flowchart
- Understand how an opportunity flowchart can identify cost-added-only steps in a process
- Be able to construct an opportunity flowchart

Section D: Deployment Flowcharts
- Know what a deployment flowchart is
- Know when to use a deployment flowchart
- Understand the types of process problems a deployment flowchart helps to identify
- Know the critical components of a deployment flowchart
- Be able to construct a deployment flowchart

INTRODUCTION

Value of Flowcharts: Background Information

Flowcharts play a key role in helping to develop **process thinking** by allowing you to

- Identify the sequence of steps needed to do a task
- Look at the relationships between the steps
- Highlight **handoffs**: places where the process flows from one person to another (these are places where problems often arise)

Process thinking creates awareness that events in the workplace are related to each other, that what happens in one step of a process can greatly affect what happens in other steps. That means people working in one part of a process must work together with people in other parts of the process so that the whole thing can flow smoothly. It also contrasts with the common belief that every situation is unique and unrelated to previous events and actions.

Flowcharts are tools that make a process visible. They expose areas where confusion or a poor arrangement of process steps can create errors, wasted effort, and excessive delays. Creating a flowchart of a process helps people

- Identify areas that need to be improved
- Work together to identify and document the best-known method for doing key process steps (this is sometimes called "standardization")
- Monitor and update the process when conditions change

In some organizations there is resistance to standardization because people think they will lose the ability to improve a process and adapt to changes. This resistance eases when people doing the work participate in establishing and documenting the best methods, and when it is understood that the methods and the documentation can be changed as process improvements are tried and confirmed.

Before flowcharting a process, people need to be clear about the **purpose** of that process. This means

- Identifying the **output** (the product or service) that the work process is designed to produce
- Identifying who uses that output (the **customers**) and what they do with it
- Understanding what happens to **inputs** such as raw materials, parts, information, or documents as they pass through the process and get transformed into the output

This guide assumes that the important work of identifying inputs, outputs, and customers, and becoming clear about the purpose of the work has already been done.

INTRODUCTION

Doing Laundry

The Problem

The Johnsons want to teach their children how to do the family laundry. They are particular about how the laundry is done and want to make sure their children follow the proper steps.

They started by having the children do the laundry with them a few times, while they explained the steps. Then they drew a diagram of the steps that the children could follow when they did the laundry on their own.

INTRODUCTION

The Value of a Diagram

How a Flowchart Helps

To create a flowchart, you have to write down the steps of a process and create a diagram that shows how those steps are related to each other.

Writing down the steps of a process

- Helps people learn the steps
- Helps make sure that everyone has the same understanding of the steps

Although a list can identify the steps, a *diagram* is often easier for people to follow and remember. Diagrams are powerful tools to help you follow a process.

SECTION A:
A Brief Guide to Flowcharts

This section is designed to help you answer the following questions. Think about the questions as you go through the section. They will be repeated at the end of the section as a quick review.

- What is a flowchart?

- What are some of the different types of flowcharts?

- What features should a good flowchart have?

- How can a flowchart help identify problems in a process?

If you can already answer these questions, you may want to go directly to one of the other sections.

SECTION A: A BRIEF GUIDE TO FLOWCHARTS

Description

Definition

A **flowchart*** is a picture of the sequence of steps in a process. Different steps or actions are represented by boxes or other symbols.

The following flowchart could be used to teach the steps in doing laundry.

- The boxes represent activities or steps
- The arrows show the sequence of steps

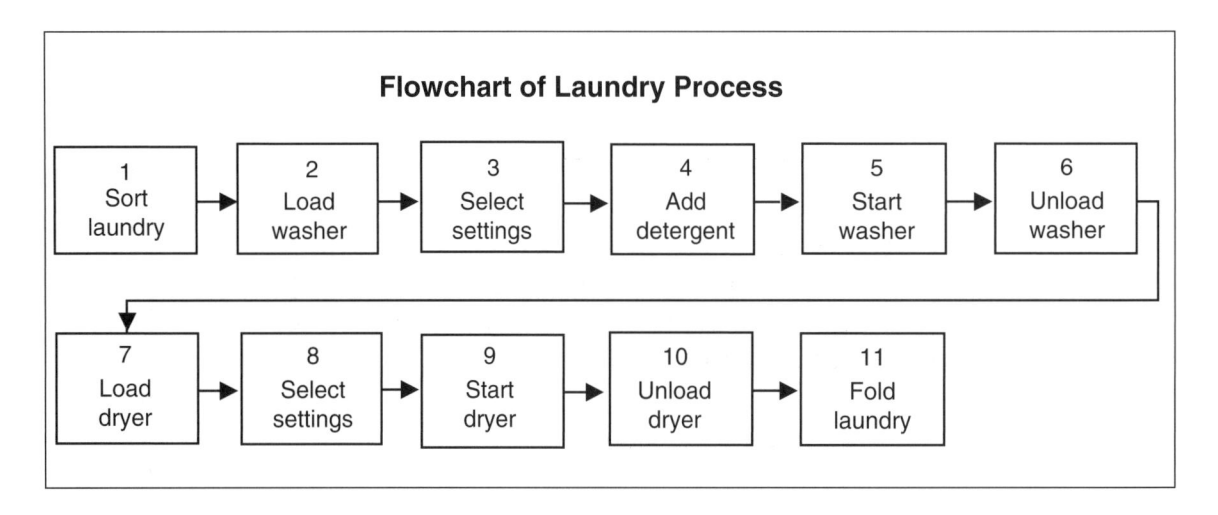

Flowchart of Laundry Process

1. Sort laundry → 2. Load washer → 3. Select settings → 4. Add detergent → 5. Start washer → 6. Unload washer →

7. Load dryer → 8. Select settings → 9. Start dryer → 10. Unload dryer → 11. Fold laundry

This flowchart shows the steps one family follows to do its laundry. A family that followed a different process would have a different flowchart. It is important that a flowchart show the steps that are actually followed, not just what someone *thinks* happens. Different families might show different levels of detail, depending on how they intend to use the flowchart.

If you have a different process for doing laundry, try to draw your own flowchart in the space below. Think about the main steps involved and write them down in sequence.

* Words in bold indicate special terms associated with these tools. Many of them can be found in the Glossary on page 113.

Flowcharts: Plain & Simple

© 2002 Oriel Incorporated. All Rights Reserved.

SECTION A: A BRIEF GUIDE TO FLOWCHARTS

What a Flowchart Shows

What It Shows

Flowcharts, such as the one for the laundry process (below), can show

- The process as a whole
- The sequence of steps
- The relationship between steps
- The beginning and ending steps, which identify the boundaries of the process

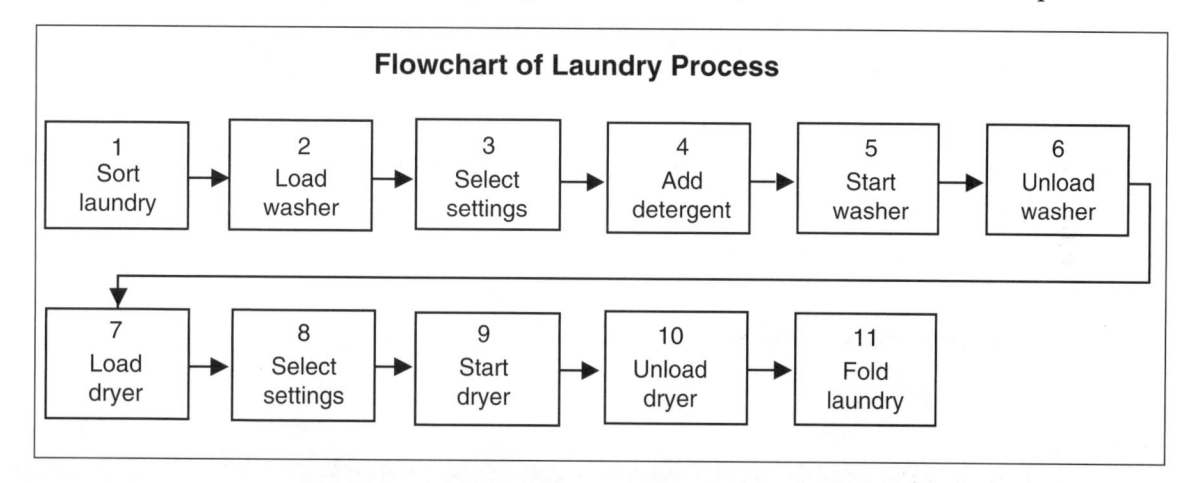

Flowchart of Laundry Process

1 Sort laundry → 2 Load washer → 3 Select settings → 4 Add detergent → 5 Start washer → 6 Unload washer →

7 Load dryer → 8 Select settings → 9 Start dryer → 10 Unload dryer → 11 Fold laundry

Use the flowchart above to answer the following questions.

1. What process is shown?

2. How many steps are there?

3. What are the beginning and ending steps in this process?

4. What steps are similar for washing and drying clothes?

5. What step comes after "Unload washer"?

Flowcharts: Plain & Simple

SECTION A: A BRIEF GUIDE TO FLOWCHARTS

What a Flowchart Shows: Answers

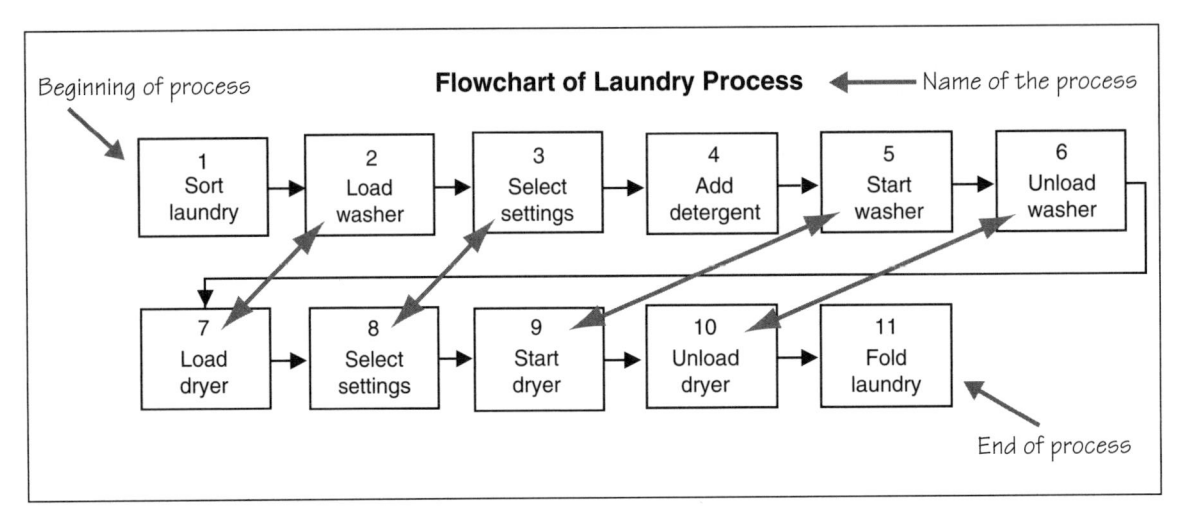

Flowchart of Laundry Process ← Name of the process

Beginning of process →

| 1 Sort laundry | 2 Load washer | 3 Select settings | 4 Add detergent | 5 Start washer | 6 Unload washer |
| 7 Load dryer | 8 Select settings | 9 Start dryer | 10 Unload dryer | 11 Fold laundry |

End of process

1. What process is shown?

    The process for doing the laundry.

2. How many steps are there?

    There are 11 steps.

3. What are the beginning and ending steps in the process?

    The process begins with sorting the laundry (Step 1) and ends with folding the laundry (Step 11).

4. What steps are similar for washing and drying clothes?

    Steps 2 and 7 are similar: Load the machine

    Steps 3 and 8 are similar: Select settings

    Steps 5 and 9 are similar: Start the machine

    Steps 6 and 10 are similar: Unload the machine

5. What step comes after "unload washer"?

    Load the dryer (Step 7) comes after unload the washer (Step 6).

SECTION A: A BRIEF GUIDE TO FLOWCHARTS

Purposes and Limitations

Purposes of Flowcharts

By requiring people to identify the sequence and relationships between the steps needed to get work done, flowcharts help

- **Build common understanding of a whole process.** This effect is biggest when a group works together to create the chart.
- **Develop process thinking.** The more that people see flowcharts, the more they become aware of how the work around them is made up of many processes that interact with each other.
- **Improve a process.** Inefficiencies can often be eliminated when people agree how a process actually works.
- **Standardize a process.** Allowing people to agree to a single set of steps for doing the work can help improve process consistency.

Limitations of Flowcharts

Flowcharts are useful tools for exposing problems in a process. But they cannot lead to improvement unless you work on solving those problems. Often this involves gathering data on the extent, impact, and causes of the problems.*

---

* For more information on other process improvement tools, see the other learning and application guides in this series.

SECTION A: A BRIEF GUIDE TO FLOWCHARTS

Flowchart Symbols

Flowcharts use different symbols to represent different kinds of process steps. It is important to standardize flowchart symbols to help others interpret and use your flowcharts.

These symbols can also be found in the **Flowcharts Quick Reminder**, packaged with this guide.

Some Standard Symbols

Use the flowchart on the next page to see how these symbols can be used. These symbols are usually included in a flowchart key to help make sure everyone understands them in the same way. Additional symbols for deployment flowcharts can be found in Section D.

Symbol	Description	Example
Start/End (oval)	**Start** and **end steps** are easier to locate if they are drawn as **ovals**.	Step 1 is the start of the process. Steps 7 and 12 are both possible endings.
Action/Task (rectangle)	**Actions** are shown in **rectangles**.	Each action that needs to be taken—such as Steps 2, 3, and 4—is written in a rectangle.
Decision (diamond)	**Decisions** are shown as **diamonds**. Each diamond should have more than one exit—for example, one path for steps taken if the decision is yes; another path if it is no.	Steps 5 and 6 are decision steps. The flow of the process changes depending on the decision that is made. If the answer to Step 6 is No, the process ends at Step 7. If the answer is Yes, the order is sent to shipping.
Sequence (arrow)	The **sequence of steps** is shown by **flowlines** with **arrows** that lead into the next flowchart symbol.	To follow the flow of the process, follow the sequence lines.
Bridge	When flowlines cross, a **bridge** helps avoid confusion by showing where each line goes.	There are no bridges in this flowchart.

12   **Flowcharts: Plain & Simple**

© 2002 Oriel Incorporated. All Rights Reserved.

SECTION A: A BRIEF GUIDE TO FLOWCHARTS

Example Showing Flowchart Symbols

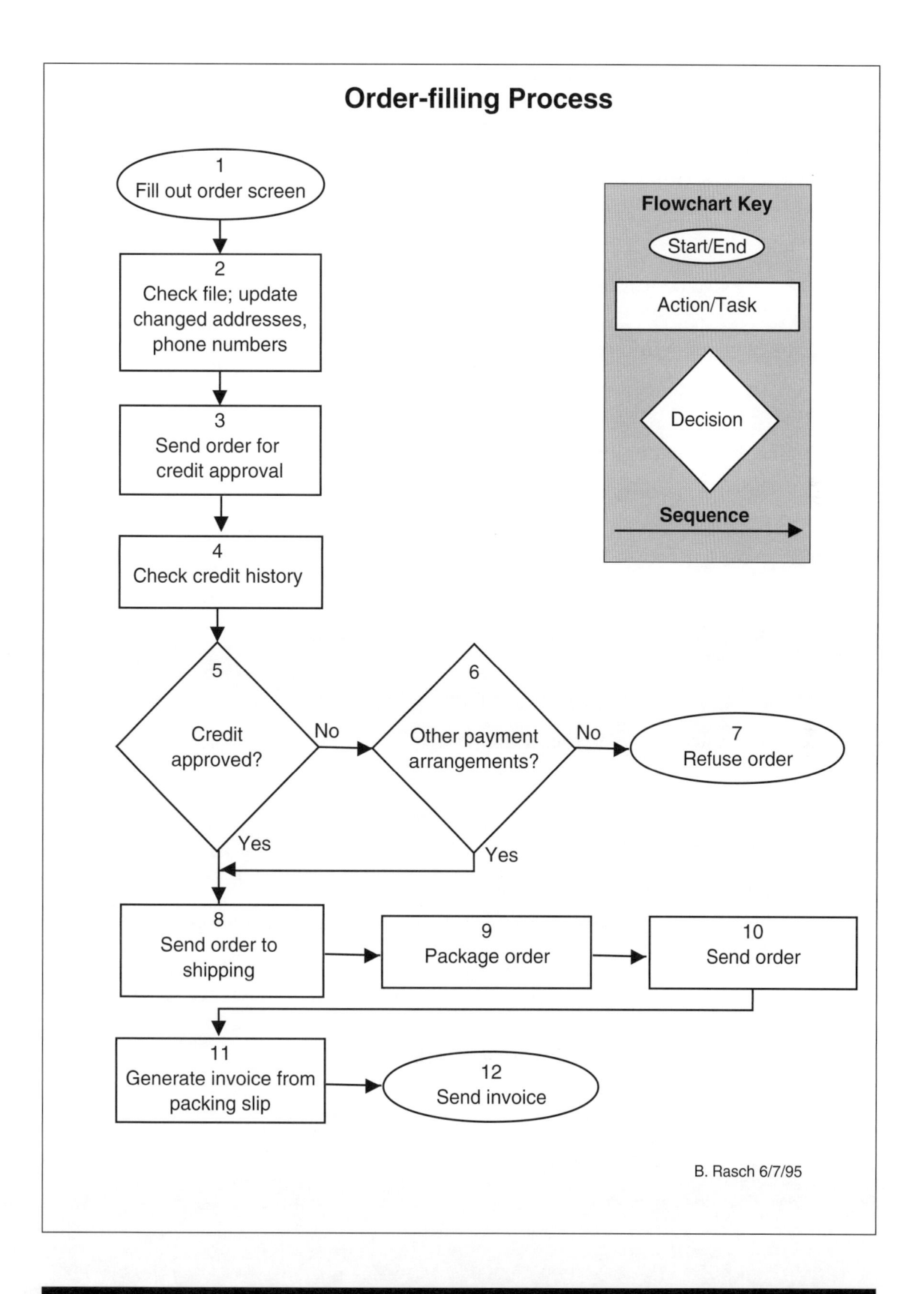

Order-filling Process

1. Fill out order screen
2. Check file; update changed addresses, phone numbers
3. Send order for credit approval
4. Check credit history
5. Credit approved?
6. Other payment arrangements?
7. Refuse order
8. Send order to shipping
9. Package order
10. Send order
11. Generate invoice from packing slip
12. Send invoice

Flowchart Key
- Start/End
- Action/Task
- Decision
- Sequence →

B. Rasch 6/7/95

Flowcharts: Plain & Simple

© 2002 Oriel Incorporated. All Rights Reserved.

SECTION A: A BRIEF GUIDE TO FLOWCHARTS

Useful Flowchart Features

Features of Good Flowcharts

The following features make it easier to use and understand a flowchart. Use this list as a checklist when you create your own flowcharts. This checklist can also be found in the **Flowcharts Quick Reminder**.

- ❒ Process name
    - To avoid confusion later

- ❒ Date of creation or update
    - To help identify the most recent version

- ❒ Name of person or group who created the chart
    - To let others know whom to contact for more information

- ❒ Clear starting and ending points
    - To help others use the chart
    - To require the creators to clarify process boundaries

- ❒ Clear direction of flow from top to bottom, left to right
    - To make it easier to follow the flow
    - To make it easier to spot process problems

- ❒ Consistent level of detail
    - To keep flowcharts appropriate for intended use
    - To avoid having steps that are at different levels of detail appear equally important

- ❒ Numbered steps
    - To make it easier to refer to specific steps

- ❒ Key of symbol definitions
    - To help others interpret the flowchart

SECTION A: A BRIEF GUIDE TO FLOWCHARTS

Example of Flowchart Features

The flowchart below was created by hotel staff trying to improve service to guests who check out at the front desk. Hotel guests had complained about service delays when they check out. The staff flowcharted the check-out process and reached agreement on the steps of the process. The result is shown below. This flowchart was their first draft and there are a few problems with the way it was drawn. Notice the features on page 14 that are included and the problems that remain.

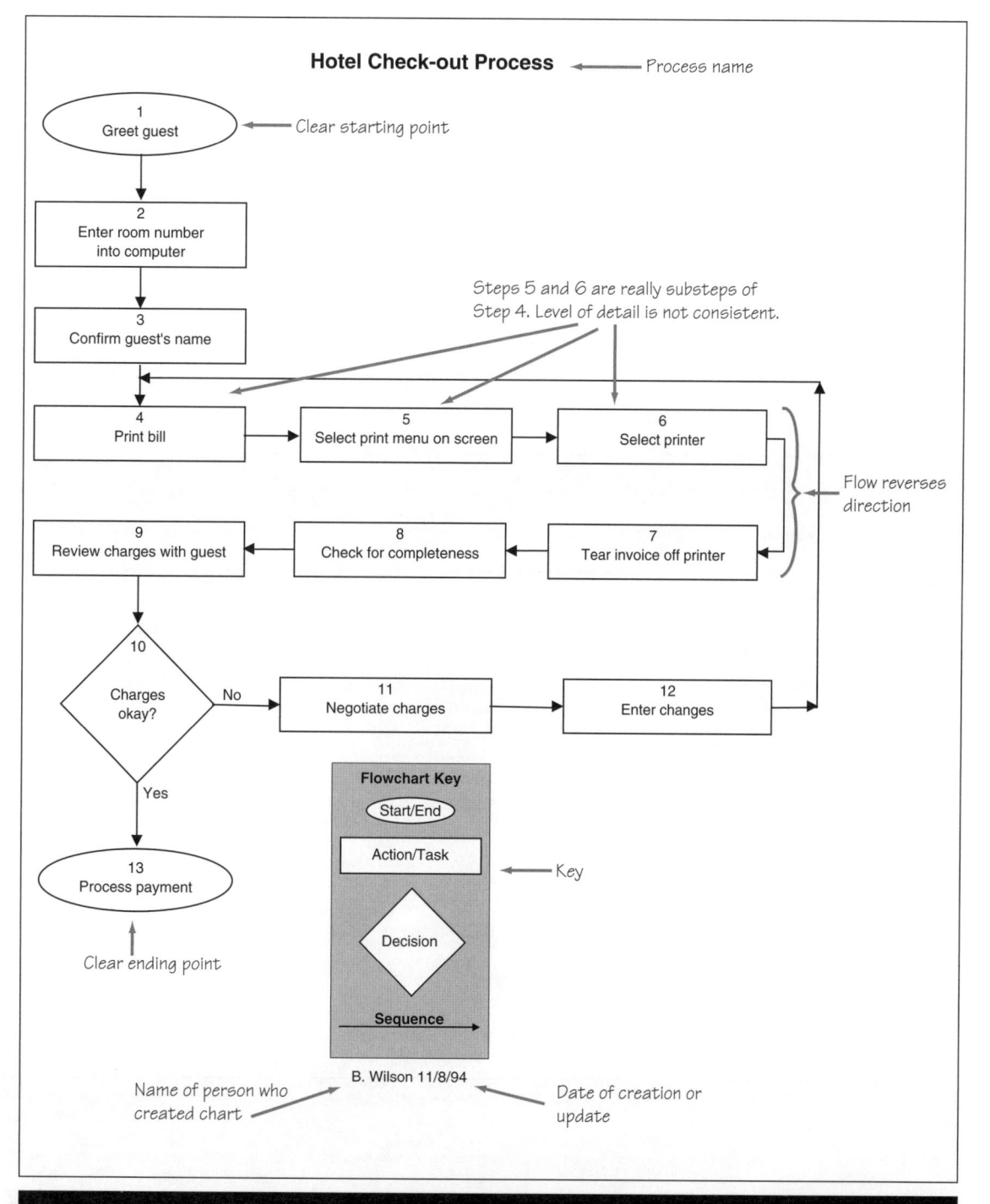

Hotel Check-out Process ← Process name

1. Greet guest ← Clear starting point
2. Enter room number into computer
3. Confirm guest's name
4. Print bill
5. Select print menu on screen
6. Select printer
7. Tear invoice off printer
8. Check for completeness
9. Review charges with guest
10. Charges okay?
11. Negotiate charges
12. Enter changes
13. Process payment

Steps 5 and 6 are really substeps of Step 4. Level of detail is not consistent.

Flow reverses direction

Clear ending point

Flowchart Key
- Start/End
- Action/Task ← Key
- Decision
- Sequence

B. Wilson 11/8/94

Name of person who created chart → ← Date of creation or update

Flowcharts: Plain & Simple

15

© 2002 Oriel Incorporated. All Rights Reserved.

SECTION A: A BRIEF GUIDE TO FLOWCHARTS

Original Hotel Example

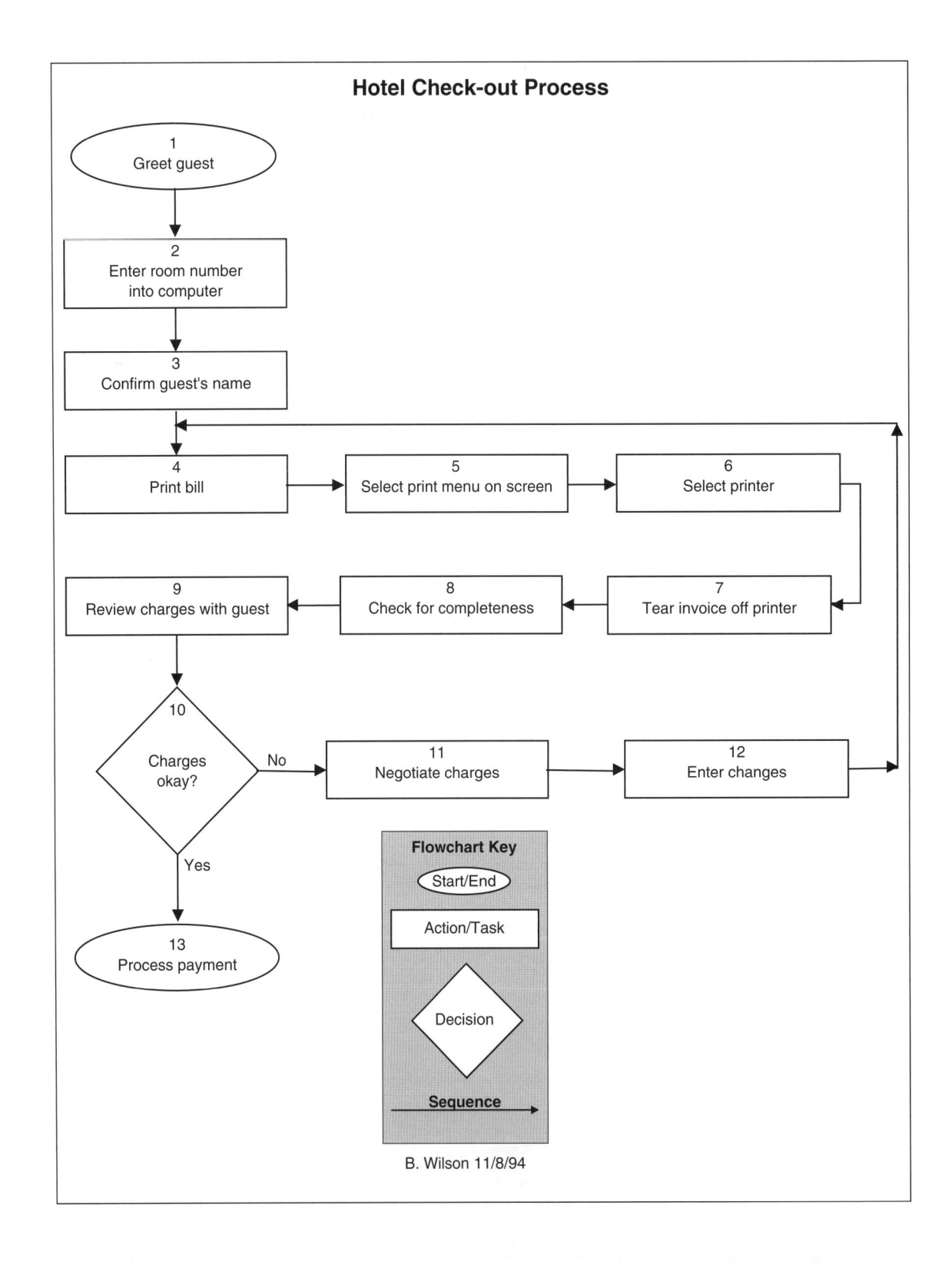

Hotel Check-out Process

1. Greet guest
2. Enter room number into computer
3. Confirm guest's name
4. Print bill
5. Select print menu on screen
6. Select printer
7. Tear invoice off printer
8. Check for completeness
9. Review charges with guest
10. Charges okay?
    - No → 11. Negotiate charges → 12. Enter changes → (back to step 3)
    - Yes → 13. Process payment

Flowchart Key
- Start/End (oval)
- Action/Task (rectangle)
- Decision (diamond)
- Sequence (arrow)

B. Wilson 11/8/94

SECTION A: A BRIEF GUIDE TO FLOWCHARTS

Revised Example of Flowchart Features

Recommendations for Improvement

In the flowchart on page 16, the flow was not clear. It zigzagged from left to right, then right to left, between Steps 4 and 10. Making sure the process flow always goes in the same direction can make the chart easier to read.

The flow from Step 12 back to Step 4 did not violate the clear direction of flow guideline. This kind of looping back occurs when there are problems in the process. Having a clear direction of flow helps these loops stand out, which helps detection of process problems.

There was also inconsistency in the level of detail in the steps. Steps 5 through 8 are really substeps of Step 4. By eliminating Steps 5 to 8, both the level of detail and clear direction problems can be fixed.

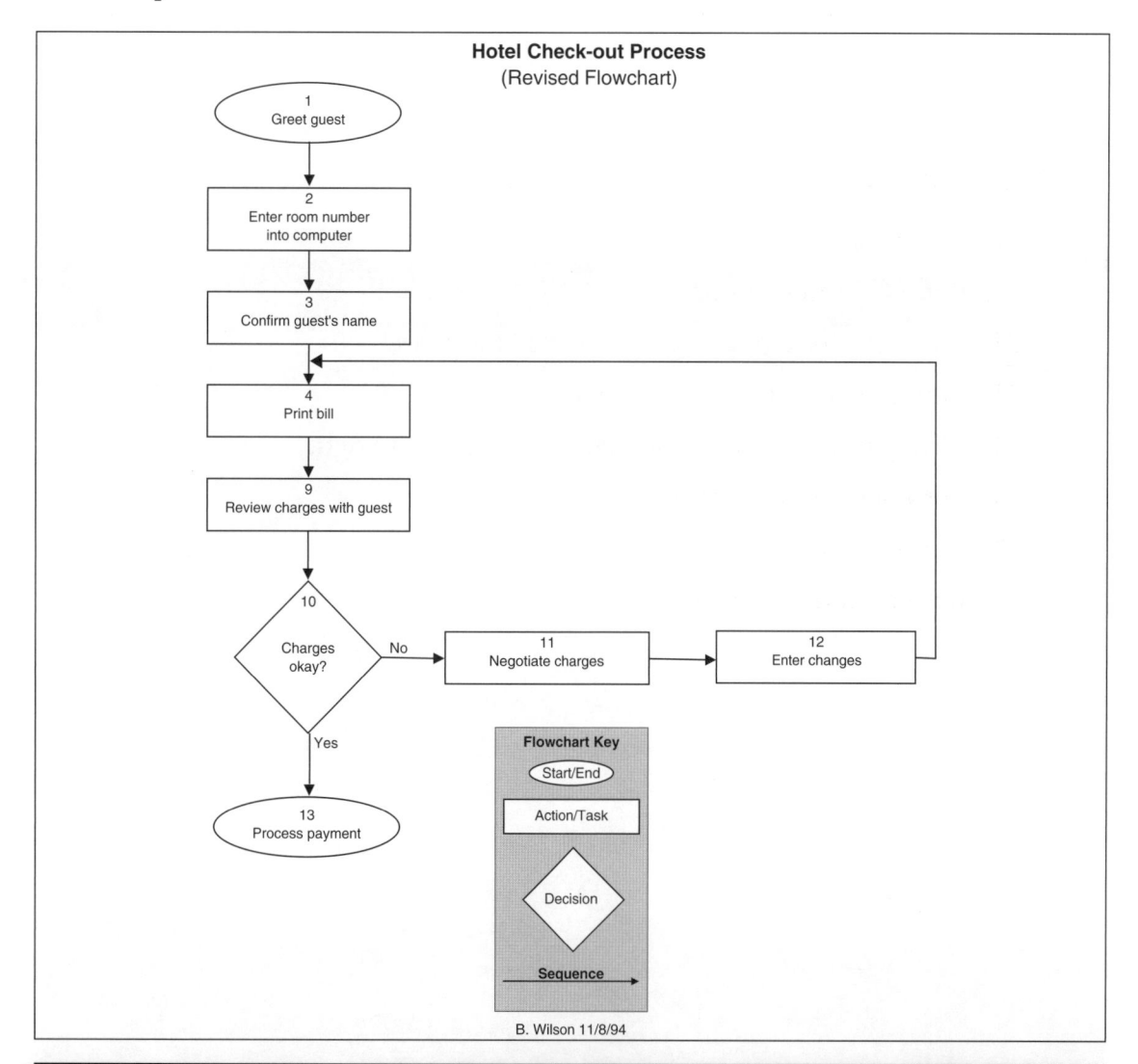

Hotel Check-out Process
(Revised Flowchart)

1. Greet guest
2. Enter room number into computer
3. Confirm guest's name
4. Print bill
9. Review charges with guest
10. Charges okay?
   - No → 11. Negotiate charges → 12. Enter changes (loops back to 4)
   - Yes → 13. Process payment

Flowchart Key
- Start/End
- Action/Task
- Decision
- Sequence

B. Wilson 11/8/94

Flowcharts: Plain & Simple 17

© 2002 Oriel Incorporated. All Rights Reserved.

Exercise 1: Construction Problems in Flowcharts

Order Entry Process Problems

Two customer service employees created the flowchart on the next page to describe the process they use to enter customer orders into the computer. They want to use this flowchart to train several new hires who will be starting soon. These two employees had never made a flowchart before and asked for suggestions to improve this flowchart.

Instructions

1. Look over the flowchart on page 19.
2. Review the checklist below on useful flowchart features.
3. Put a check next to each item on the checklist if the item is in the flowchart.
4. Review the unchecked items. These are construction problems in the flowchart.

Checklist of Useful Flowchart Features

- ❐ Process name
- ❐ Date of creation or update
- ❐ Name of person or group who created the chart
- ❐ Clear starting and ending points
- ❐ Clear direction of flow from top to bottom, left to right
- ❐ Consistent level of detail
- ❐ Numbered steps
- ❐ Key of symbol definitions

EXERCISE 1: CONSTRUCTION PROBLEMS IN FLOWCHARTS

Construction Problems Example

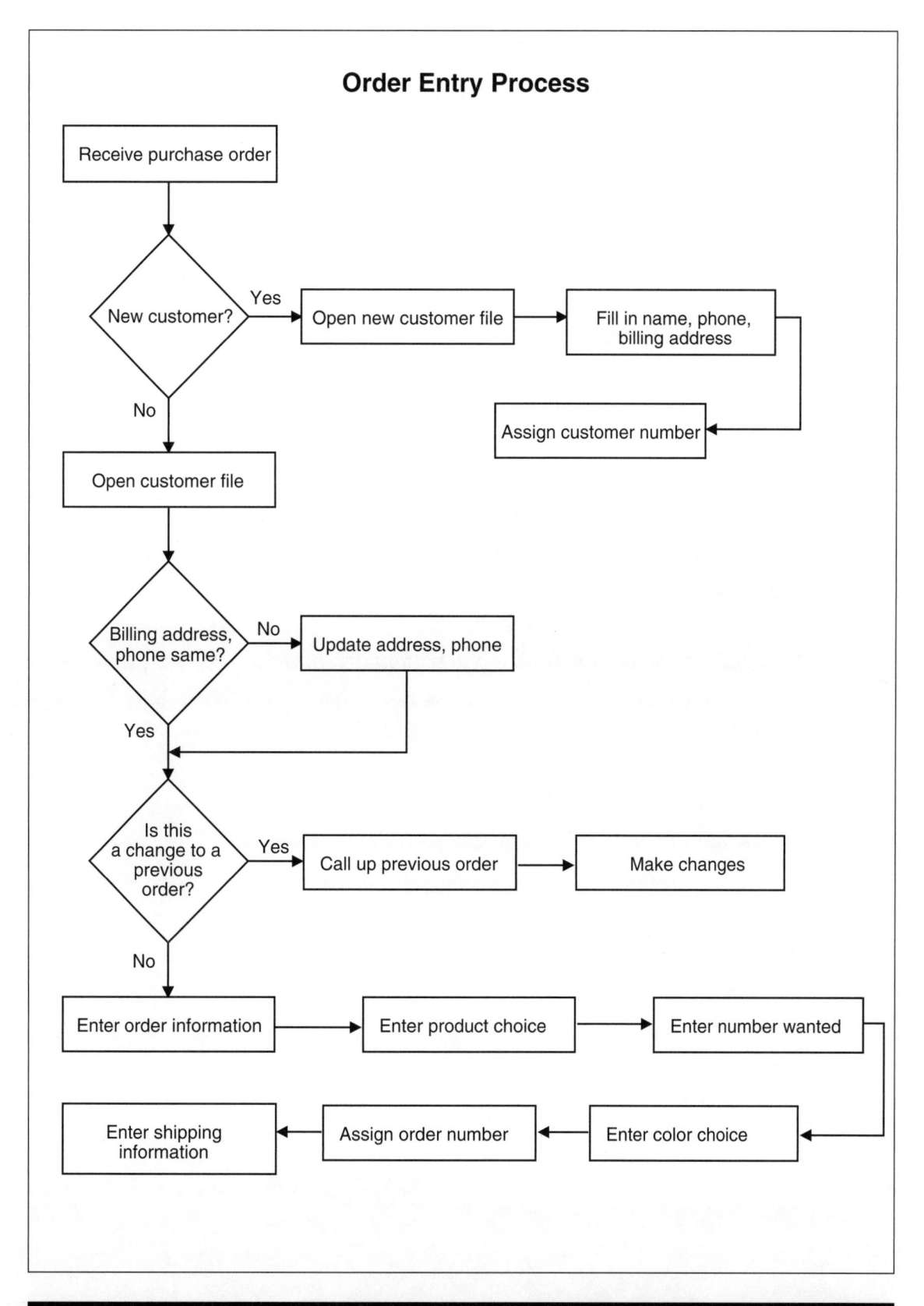

Order Entry Process

```
Receive purchase order
         │
         ▼
   New customer? ──Yes──▶ Open new customer file ──▶ Fill in name, phone, billing address
         │                                                        │
         No                                                       ▼
         │                                              Assign customer number
         ▼
   Open customer file
         │
         ▼
   Billing address, ──No──▶ Update address, phone
   phone same?                       │
         │                           │
        Yes◀──────────────────────────┘
         │
         ▼
   Is this a change
   to a previous ──Yes──▶ Call up previous order ──▶ Make changes
   order?
         │
         No
         ▼
   Enter order information ──▶ Enter product choice ──▶ Enter number wanted
                                                                │
                                                                ▼
   Enter shipping  ◀── Assign order number ◀── Enter color choice
   information
```

Flowcharts: Plain & Simple   19

© 2002 Oriel Incorporated. All Rights Reserved.

EXERCISE 1: CONSTRUCTION PROBLEMS IN FLOWCHARTS

Construction Problems: Answers

Checklist for Order Entry Process Flowchart

Only one of the eight useful flowchart features should be checked. The others are missing completely or are inconsistent.

- ☑ Process name
  - Flowchart is titled "Order Entry Process"

- ☐ Date of creation or update
  - The date is missing

- ☐ Name of person or group who created the chart
  - Creator's name is missing

- ☐ Clear starting and ending points
  - Start and end points are unclear
  - Three boxes have no exit so it is not clear if they are endpoints or errors

- ☐ Clear direction of flow from top to bottom, left to right
  - The process flow reverses direction twice, zigzagging left to right then right to left

- ☐ Consistent level of detail
  - Details are provided for some steps and not for others
  - Three activities near the end are really substeps of "Enter order information"

- ☐ Numbered steps
  - Steps are not numbered

- ☐ Key of symbol definitions
  - Key is missing

EXERCISE 1: CONSTRUCTION PROBLEMS IN FLOWCHARTS

Construction Problems Flowchart

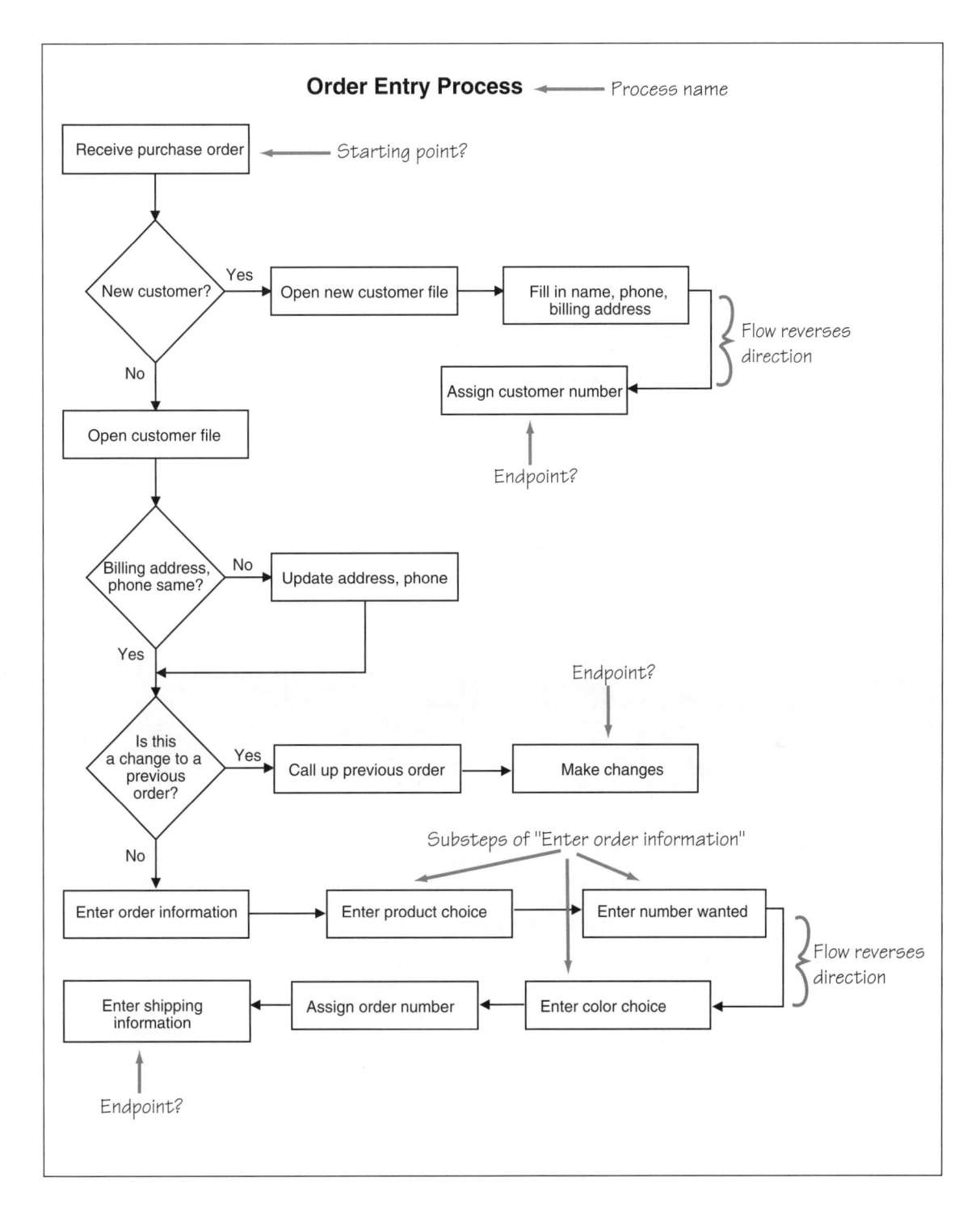

Order Entry Process ← *Process name*

- Receive purchase order ← *Starting point?*
- New customer?
  - Yes → Open new customer file → Fill in name, phone, billing address → Assign customer number *(Flow reverses direction)* ← *Endpoint?*
  - No → Open customer file
- Billing address, phone same?
  - No → Update address, phone
  - Yes ↓
- Is this a change to a previous order?
  - Yes → Call up previous order → Make changes ← *Endpoint?*
  - No ↓
- Enter order information → Enter product choice → Enter number wanted → Enter color choice → Assign order number → Enter shipping information ← *Endpoint?*

Substeps of "Enter order information"

Flow reverses direction

You can find a corrected version of this flowchart on page 23.

Flowcharts: Plain & Simple — 21

© 2002 Oriel Incorporated. All Rights Reserved.

EXERCISE 1: CONSTRUCTION PROBLEMS IN FLOWCHARTS

Construction Improvements

The flowchart on the next page shows some changes that improved the Order Entry Flowchart.

- The creation date was added
- The name of the creator was added
- The start and end points are clearly indicated by ovals
- The end point is the only shape without an exit
- Flow is clear from top to bottom, left to right
- A bridge between Steps 11 and 12 keeps the flow clear
- Level of detail is consistent; substeps of "Enter order information" have been eliminated
- Steps are numbered
- A key was added

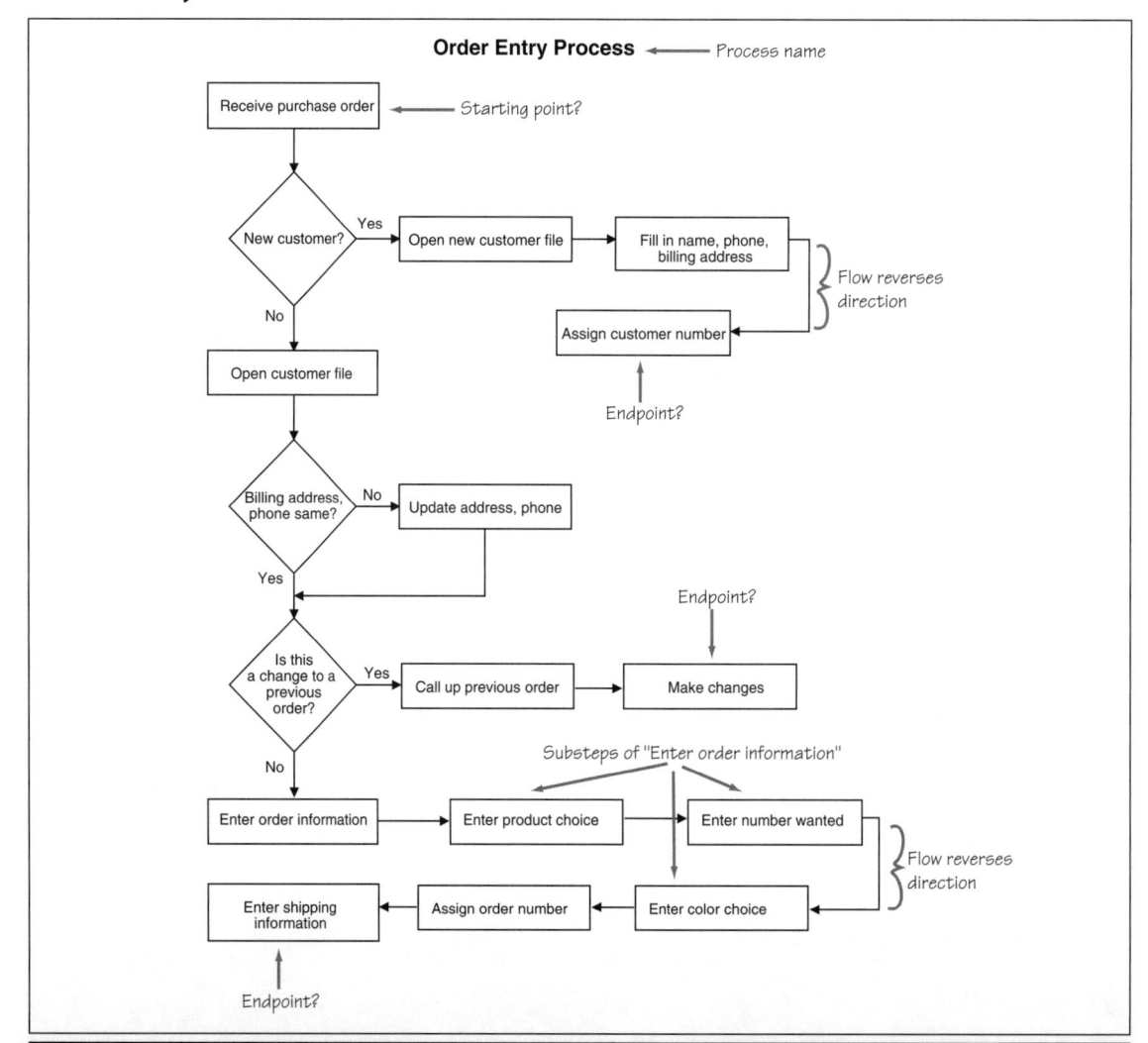

Order Entry Process ← Process name

Receive purchase order ← Starting point?

New customer?
- Yes → Open new customer file → Fill in name, phone, billing address → Assign customer number (Flow reverses direction) ← Endpoint?
- No → Open customer file

Billing address, phone same?
- No → Update address, phone
- Yes

Is this a change to a previous order?
- Yes → Call up previous order → Make changes ← Endpoint?
- No

Substeps of "Enter order information":
Enter order information → Enter product choice → Enter number wanted → Enter color choice ← Assign order number ← Enter shipping information (Flow reverses direction)

↑ Endpoint?

22   **Flowcharts: Plain & Simple**

© 2002 Oriel Incorporated. All Rights Reserved.

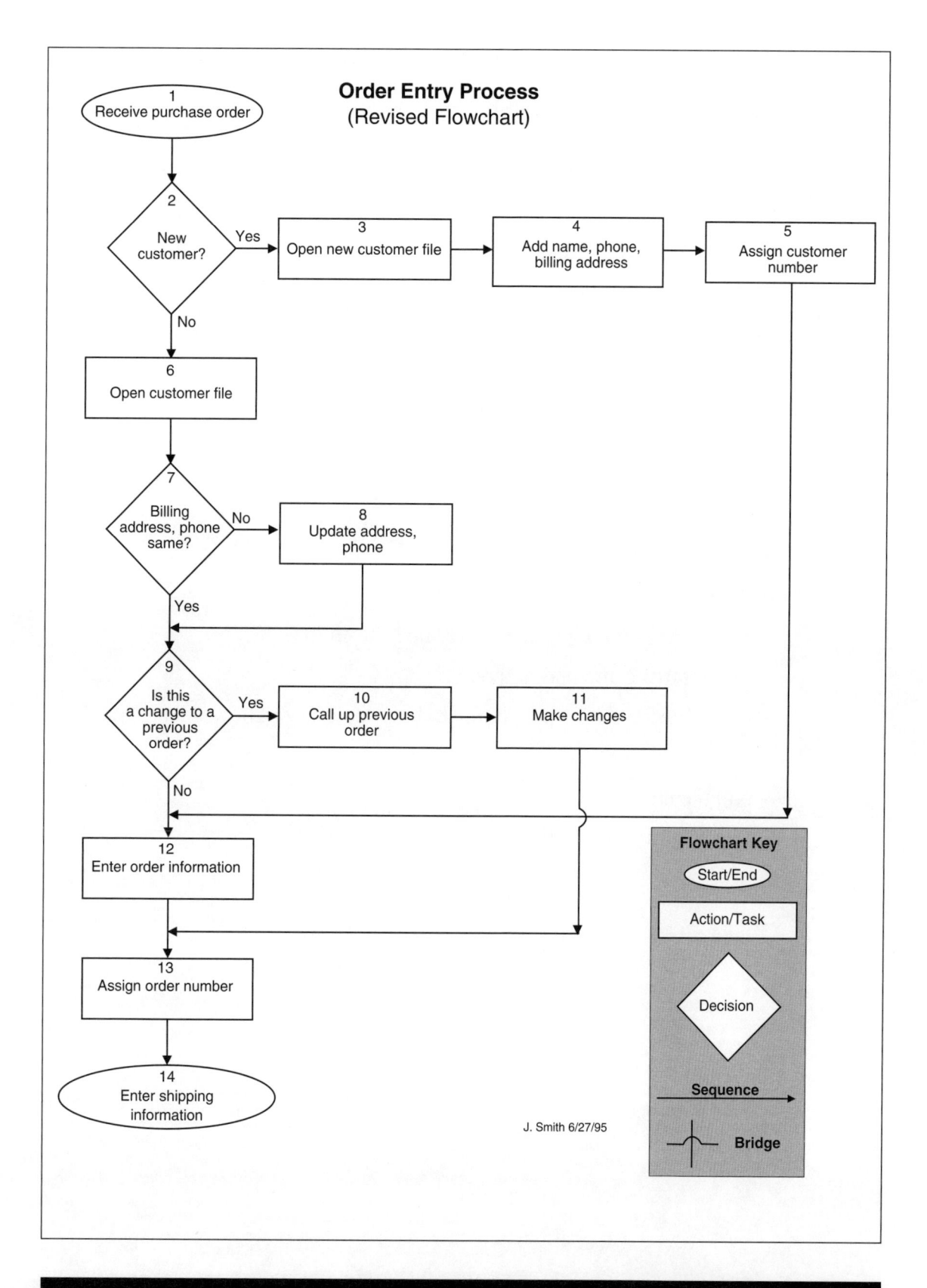

EXERCISE 1: CONSTRUCTION PROBLEMS IN FLOWCHARTS

Revised Flowchart

Order Entry Process
(Revised Flowchart)

1. Receive purchase order
2. New customer? — Yes → 3. Open new customer file → 4. Add name, phone, billing address → 5. Assign customer number
2. No →
6. Open customer file
7. Billing address, phone same? — No → 8. Update address, phone
7. Yes →
9. Is this a change to a previous order? — Yes → 10. Call up previous order → 11. Make changes
9. No →
12. Enter order information
13. Assign order number
14. Enter shipping information

J. Smith 6/27/95

Flowchart Key
- Start/End
- Action/Task
- Decision
- Sequence
- Bridge

Flowcharts: Plain & Simple

EXERCISE 1: CONSTRUCTION PROBLEMS IN FLOWCHARTS

SUMMARY: Exercise 1

Key Points About Creating Useful Flowcharts

This exercise showed a flowchart for the process that customer service employees used to enter orders into the computer. The initial flowchart lacked most of the features that should be included for a flowchart to be useful. For this reason, it was difficult to follow.

By revising the flowchart to incorporate useful flowchart features, the order entry process became easier to follow and understand. The beginning, end, and flow of the process were clear. If there were still questions, the name of the creator was included, along with numbered steps to make any discussion of the process easier.

The main things you should remember from this exercise are

- Creating a useful flowchart requires attention to details.
- To be useful, flowcharts need more information than just the sequence of steps. They should include
    — Process name
    — Date of creation or update
    — Name of person or group who created the chart
    — Clear starting and ending points
    — Clear direction of flow from top to bottom, left to right
    — Consistent level of detail
    — Numbered steps
    — Key of symbol definitions

Types of Flowcharts

Three Types Of Flowcharts

There are many types of flowcharts that serve a variety of purposes. The flowcharts covered in this book are those used most often to look at the flow of work in an organization in order to understand, standardize, and improve work processes.

- Basic flowcharts (including detailed flowcharts)
    - Show the steps taken in a process

- Opportunity flowcharts
    - Show the steps taken in a process
    - Distinguish between steps taken when things go right and steps taken when things go wrong

- Deployment flowcharts
    - Show who does which steps in a process
    - Show where work flows from one function to another

SECTION A: A BRIEF GUIDE TO FLOWCHARTS

Basic Flowcharts

Basic flowcharts show the sequence of steps in a job or process. There are different types of basic flowcharts, depending on how much detail is needed.

1. Basic Flowchart With Major Steps

This flowchart can be used to show customers the main steps in a painting project.

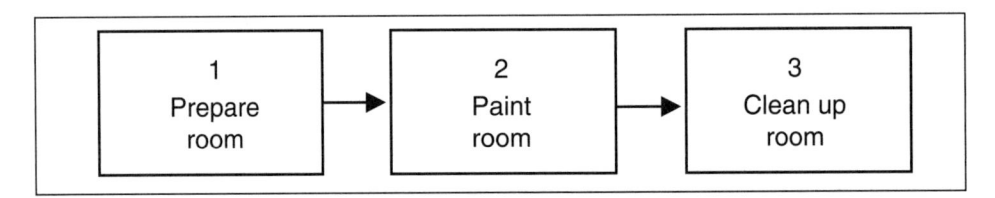

```
┌──────────┐    ┌──────────┐    ┌──────────┐
│    1     │    │    2     │    │    3     │
│ Prepare  │ ─► │  Paint   │ ─► │ Clean up │
│  room    │    │  room    │    │  room    │
└──────────┘    └──────────┘    └──────────┘
```

2. Basic Top-Down Flowchart

Top-down flowcharts show both the major steps in a process and the next level of substeps. The main flow of the process is shown by the sequence of major steps across the top of the picture. Substeps are listed below each major step.

Top-down flowcharts are particularly useful for identifying the substeps in a process.

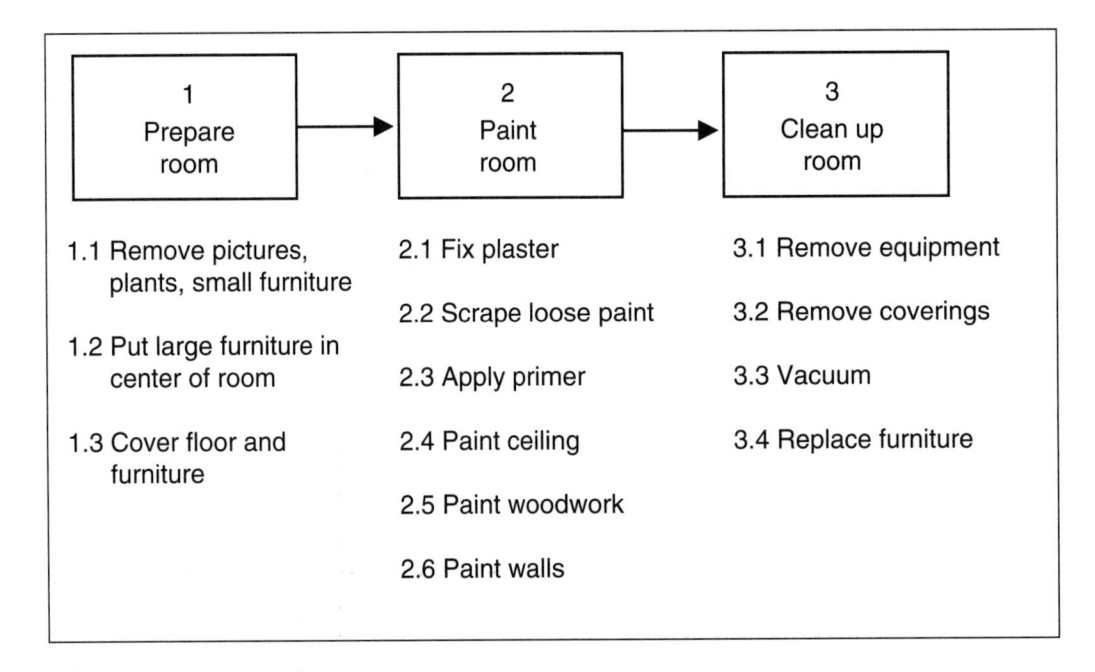

```
┌──────────┐    ┌──────────┐    ┌──────────┐
│    1     │    │    2     │    │    3     │
│ Prepare  │ ─► │  Paint   │ ─► │ Clean up │
│  room    │    │  room    │    │  room    │
└──────────┘    └──────────┘    └──────────┘
```

1.1 Remove pictures, plants, small furniture	2.1 Fix plaster	3.1 Remove equipment
	2.2 Scrape loose paint	3.2 Remove coverings
1.2 Put large furniture in center of room	2.3 Apply primer	3.3 Vacuum
1.3 Cover floor and furniture	2.4 Paint ceiling	3.4 Replace furniture
	2.5 Paint woodwork	
	2.6 Paint walls	

SECTION A: A BRIEF GUIDE TO FLOWCHARTS

Detailed Flowcharts

3. Basic Flowchart With Detailed Steps

Basic flowcharts with detailed steps (also called **detailed flowcharts**) can be used to learn more about how a process works. The flowchart below might be used in scheduling workers for a job. The labels along the left side show the relationship between this flowchart and the flowcharts on page 26.

The detailed flowchart is the only type of basic flowchart covered in greater depth in this guide because it is one of the most commonly used flowcharts. Detailed flowcharts are covered in greater depth in Section B, beginning on page 35.

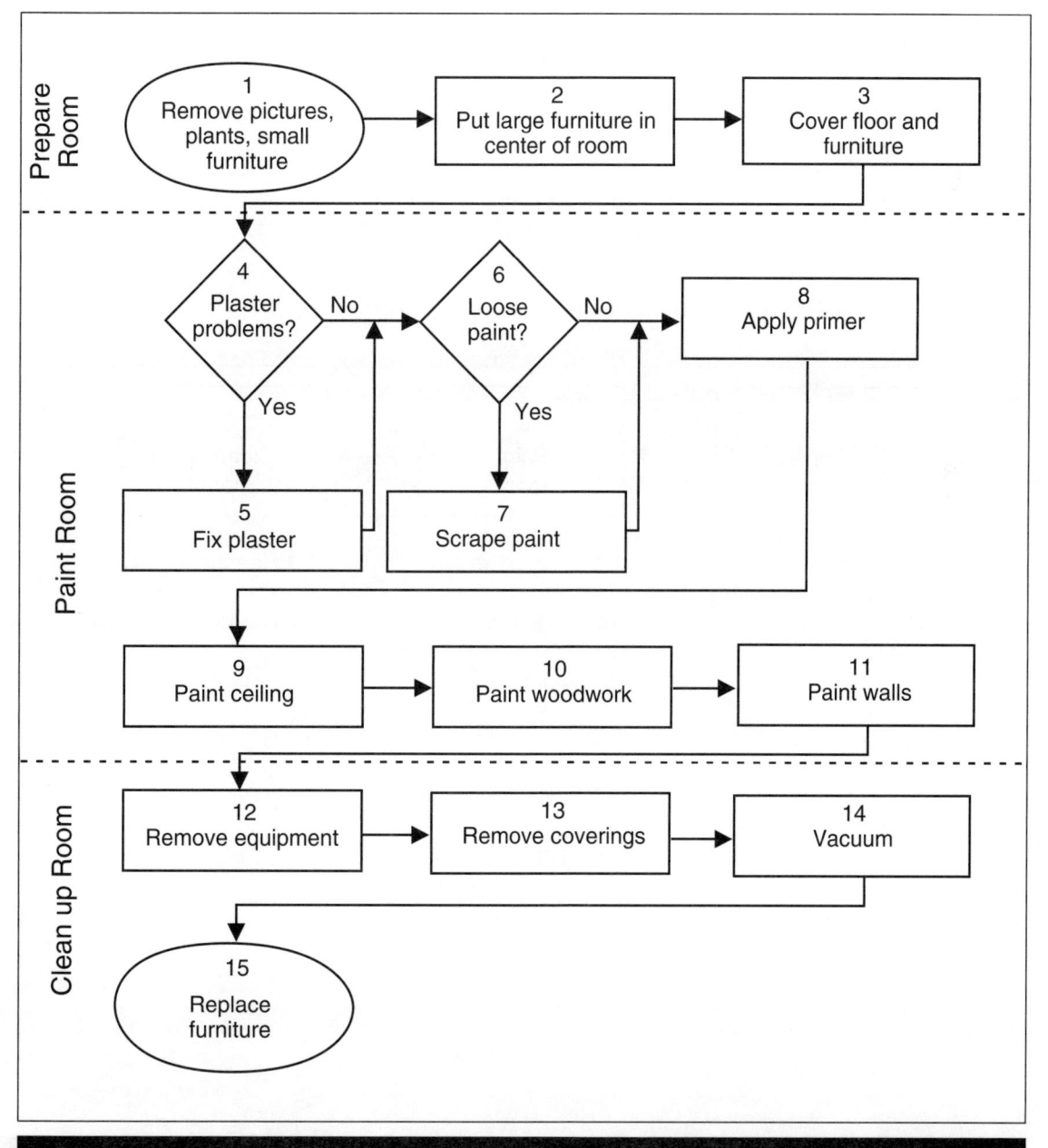

Prepare Room
1. Remove pictures, plants, small furniture
2. Put large furniture in center of room
3. Cover floor and furniture

Paint Room
4. Plaster problems? — No → 6. Loose paint? — No → 8. Apply primer
5. Fix plaster (Yes from 4)
7. Scrape paint (Yes from 6)
9. Paint ceiling
10. Paint woodwork
11. Paint walls

Clean up Room
12. Remove equipment
13. Remove coverings
14. Vacuum
15. Replace furniture

Flowcharts: Plain & Simple

© 2002 Oriel Incorporated. All Rights Reserved.

SECTION A: A BRIEF GUIDE TO FLOWCHARTS

Opportunity Flowcharts

Description

Opportunity flowcharts are organized to separate steps taken when things go right from steps taken when things go wrong.

- **Value-added** steps are needed when things go correctly. They move down the left side of the chart.

- **Cost-added-only** steps are taken when things go wrong. They flow across the right side of the chart.

- If there were no problems, the process would flow down the left side of the page.

Reading an Opportunity Flowchart

The flowchart on the next page divides the steps in the painting process into those that have to be done all the time and those that are taken when things go wrong.

- Steps in the left-hand column are value-added steps (Steps 1, 6, 7, 9, 12, 13, 16, and 19). They would all need to be done even if no mistakes were made.

- The shaded steps (Steps 2, 8, 10, 14, and 17) are decision steps that inspect for mistakes. Each diamond leads to steps needed to remedy the problem.

- Step 3 is a decision step, but it does not inspect for mistakes. It is a response to the problem identified in Step 2, so it is also cost-added-only.

- Step 6 is a decision step, but it is not a cost-added-only step. It needs to be done even when there are no problems with the process because plaster problems were probably there before the painters began their work. This decision is part of the value-added process.

Opportunity flowcharts are covered in greater detail in Section C, beginning on page 55.

SECTION A: A BRIEF GUIDE TO FLOWCHARTS

Painting a Room: Opportunity Flowchart

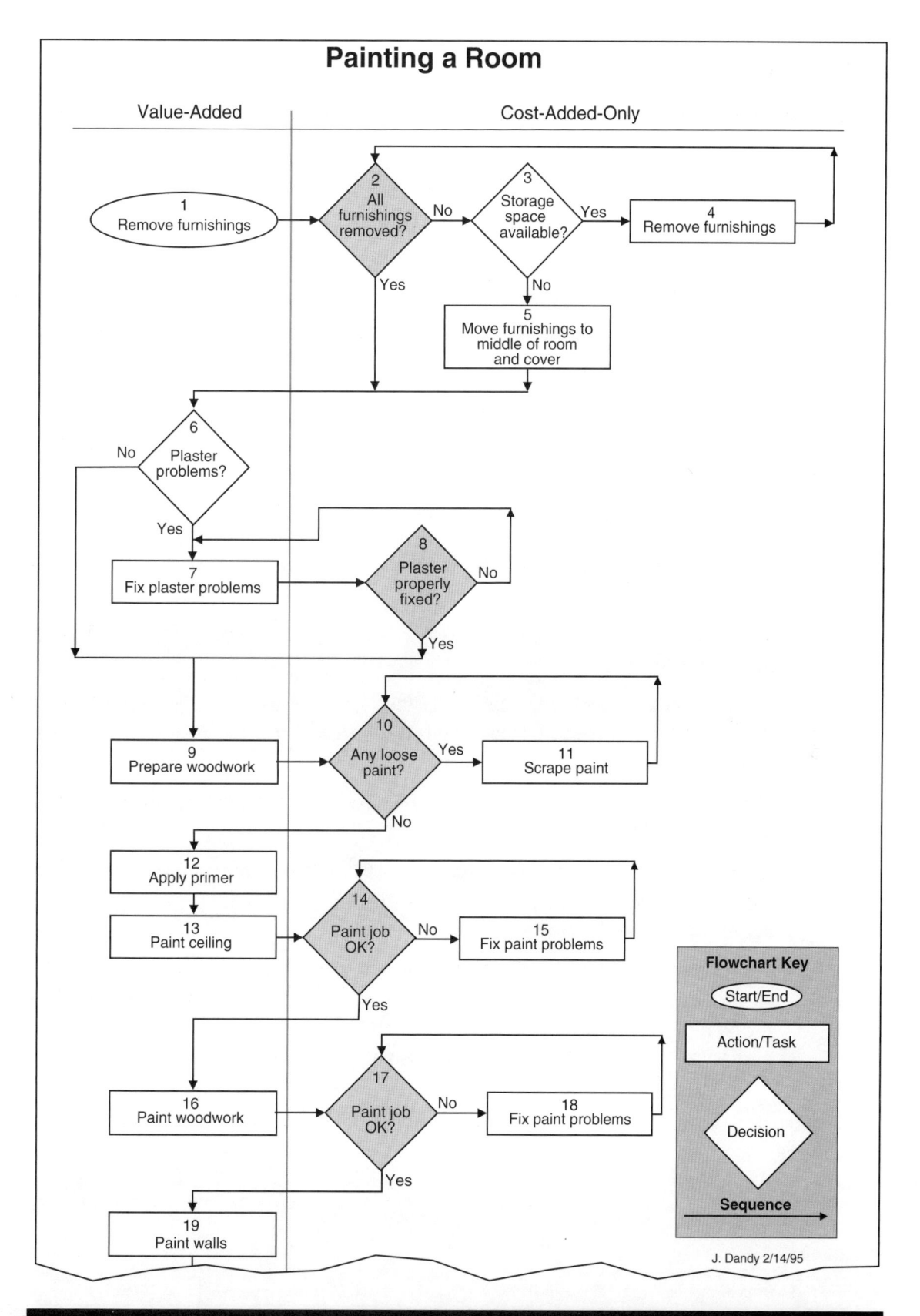

Painting a Room

Value-Added | **Cost-Added-Only**

1. Remove furnishings
2. All furnishings removed?
3. Storage space available?
4. Remove furnishings
5. Move furnishings to middle of room and cover
6. Plaster problems?
7. Fix plaster problems
8. Plaster properly fixed?
9. Prepare woodwork
10. Any loose paint?
11. Scrape paint
12. Apply primer
13. Paint ceiling
14. Paint job OK?
15. Fix paint problems
16. Paint woodwork
17. Paint job OK?
18. Fix paint problems
19. Paint walls

Flowchart Key
- Start/End
- Action/Task
- Decision
- Sequence

J. Dandy 2/14/95

Flowcharts: Plain & Simple — 29

© 2002 Oriel Incorporated. All Rights Reserved.

SECTION A: A BRIEF GUIDE TO FLOWCHARTS

Deployment Flowcharts

Description

Deployment flowcharts show the detailed steps in a process and which people or group are involved in each step.

- People or groups involved are listed across the top of the chart
- Steps are listed in the columns of the people who carry them out or who are in charge
- Time flows down the page; any steps pictured in parallel occur at the same time
- **Handoffs**, where work moves from one person or group to another, are shown by horizontal lines connecting one column to another
- The action/task box is in the column of the person in charge of that step
- The assist symbol (○———) means the person is involved but not in charge

Reading a Deployment Flowchart

The flowchart on the next page divides the steps in the painting process according to who is involved in each step.

- The painter is responsible for Steps 1, 2, 3, 5, 7, and 10. These steps are all listed in his column.
- The assistant helps the painter with Steps 1, 2, 5, 7, and 10. The steps are shown in the painter's column because he is in charge, but an assist circle is drawn in the assistant's column.
- The assistant is in charge of Steps 4, 6, 8, and 9. These steps are all listed in the assistant's column.
- Steps 3 and 4 are done at the same time. While the painter prepares the woodwork, the assistant paints the ceiling. This is shown by placing the two action boxes side by side.
- The painter hands off work to the assistant after Steps 2, 5, and 7. The assistant cannot start painting the ceiling (Step 4) until the painter finishes fixing plaster problems (Step 2). Horizontal lines, like the one connecting Step 2 in the painter's column with Step 4 in the assistant's column, signal a handoff.

Deployment flowcharts are covered in greater detail in Section D, beginning on page 81.

SECTION A: A BRIEF GUIDE TO FLOWCHARTS

Painting a Room: Deployment Flowchart

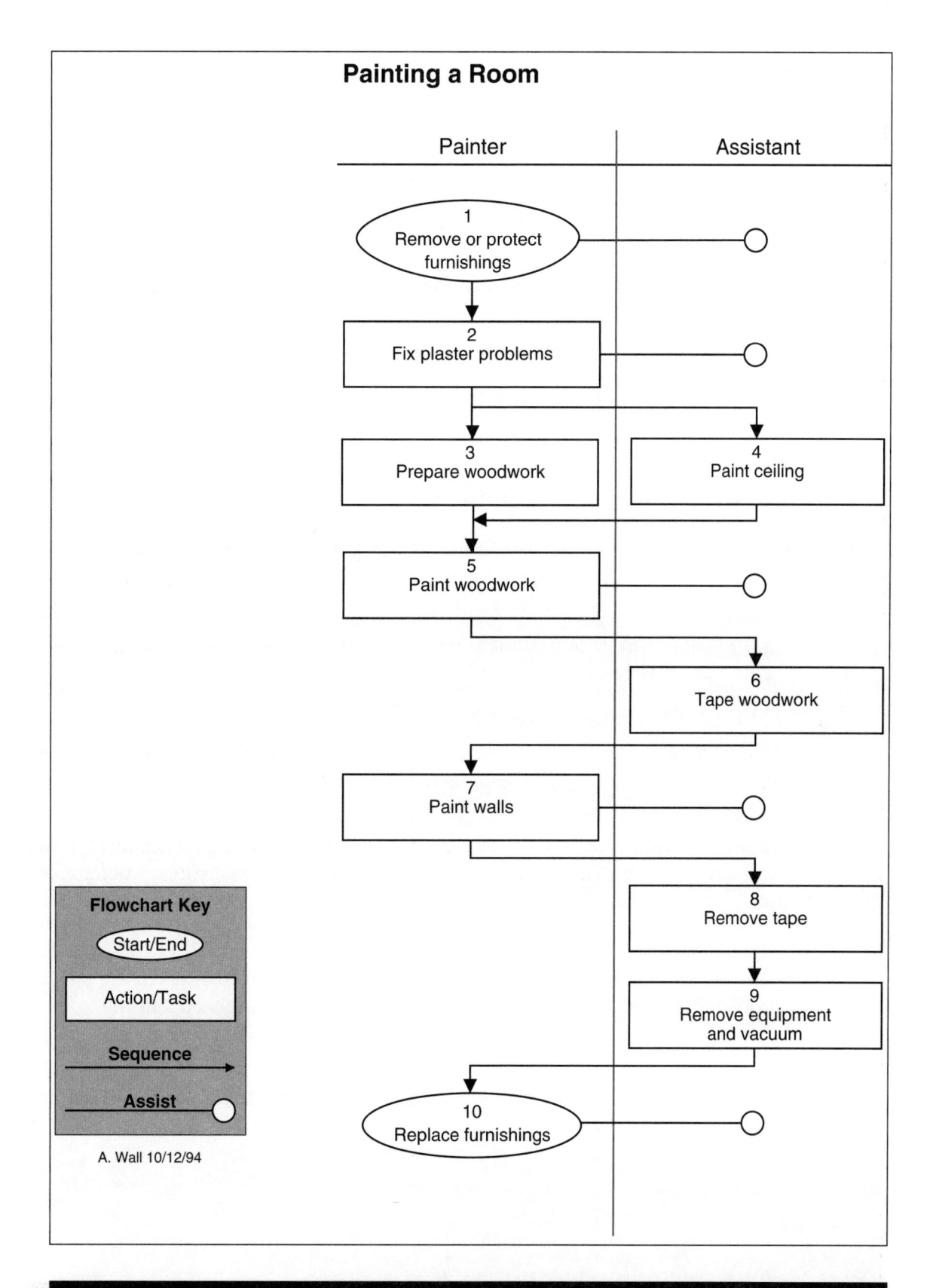

Painting a Room

Painter	Assistant

1. Remove or protect furnishings
2. Fix plaster problems
3. Prepare woodwork
4. Paint ceiling
5. Paint woodwork
6. Tape woodwork
7. Paint walls
8. Remove tape
9. Remove equipment and vacuum
10. Replace furnishings

Flowchart Key
- Start/End
- Action/Task
- Sequence
- Assist

A. Wall 10/12/94

Flowcharts: Plain & Simple

SECTION A: A BRIEF GUIDE TO FLOWCHARTS

How Much Detail

Amount of Detail

The amount of detail you include on a flowchart depends on how you want to use it.

- Flowcharts that show only the major process steps are useful when trying to quickly capture the basic outline of a process. They show
  - Only the main steps of the process

- Flowcharts with detailed steps are useful when trying to improve or standardize a process. They show
  - The sequence and relationship of steps
  - Different types of actions with differently shaped boxes
  - Steps taken when things go wrong

Guidelines for Amount of Detail

The more detail you capture, the more information you have about how a process actually works. However, if you have too much detail, users can get bogged down. Finding the right balance is not always easy.

- Lots of detail can be important when it is absolutely necessary that the work is done exactly the same each time.
- Only include as much detail as you think you need.
- Capturing a lot of detail takes time and requires resources. These are costs that have to be balanced by the benefits of the flowchart.

If you are unsure how much detail is needed, start with less detail. You can always add more detail later on when you know where a lack of specifics has created problems or confusion.

When to Use Which Flowchart

Tips on When to Use Which Type of Flowchart

When you want	Use
A quick outline of the big steps in a process	Basic flowchart with major steps
A deep look at a process that involves mostly one person or group	Basic flowchart with detailed steps
A quick list of both big steps and substeps	Top-down flowchart
To understand or improve a process involving handoffs among several people or groups	Deployment flowchart
To understand or improve a process that has a lot of rework, inspections, approvals, missing parts, or missing information	Opportunity flowchart

This table can also be found in the **Flowcharts Quick Reminder** packaged with this guide.

SECTION A: A BRIEF GUIDE TO FLOWCHARTS

Section A: Quick Check

Review of Key Questions

Here are the questions listed at the beginning of this section. Check to make sure you can answer them. If you aren't sure about any of the answers, you may want to review this section before you continue.

- What is a flowchart?

- What are some of the different types of flowcharts?

- What features should a good flowchart have?

- How can a flowchart help identify problems in a process?

For More Information

Each of the three types of flowcharts introduced in this section is described in more detail later in this guide. You can work through all these sections at once or go directly to the section that covers the type of flowchart you think will be most useful to you.

- Detailed flowcharts, go to page 35
- Opportunity flowcharts, go to page 55
- Deployment flowcharts, go to page 81

SECTION B:
Detailed Flowcharts

This section is designed to help you answer the following questions. Think about the questions as you go through the section. They will be repeated at the end of the section as a quick review.

- What is a detailed flowchart?

- When would I use a detailed flowchart?

- How can I use a detailed flowchart to help identify process problems?

- What are the critical components of a detailed flowchart?

- What steps are needed to create a detailed flowchart?

SECTION B: DETAILED FLOWCHARTS

Detailed Flowcharts

Definition

Detailed flowcharts are one type of basic flowchart. They break the sequence of steps in a job or process down into detailed substeps.

A review of detailed flowcharts can be found in the **Flowcharts Quick Reminder**.

Reading a Detailed Flowchart

Use the flowchart for fixing a bike on the next page to answer the following questions.

1. Which steps are the start and end points?

2. Which steps are action steps?

3. Which steps are decisions?

4. Step 2 asks, "Do you have a pump?"

    a) If you do not have a pump, what step comes next?

    b) If you do have a pump, what step comes next?

SECTION B: DETAILED FLOWCHARTS

Detailed Flowchart Example

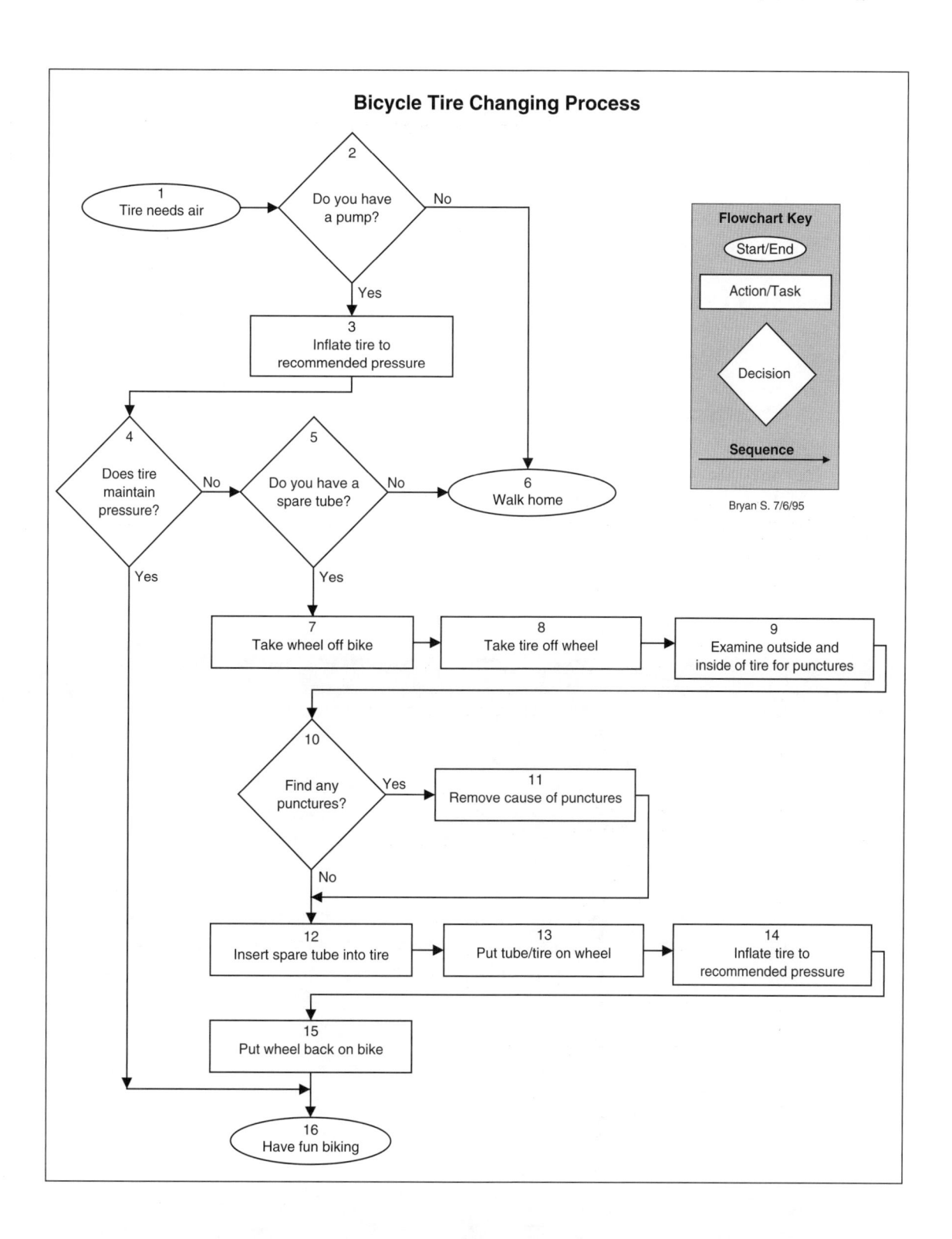

Bicycle Tire Changing Process

1. Tire needs air
2. Do you have a pump?
   - No → 6. Walk home
   - Yes → 3
3. Inflate tire to recommended pressure
4. Does tire maintain pressure?
   - Yes → 16
   - No → 5
5. Do you have a spare tube?
   - No → 6. Walk home
   - Yes → 7
6. Walk home
7. Take wheel off bike
8. Take tire off wheel
9. Examine outside and inside of tire for punctures
10. Find any punctures?
    - Yes → 11
    - No → 12
11. Remove cause of punctures
12. Insert spare tube into tire
13. Put tube/tire on wheel
14. Inflate tire to recommended pressure
15. Put wheel back on bike
16. Have fun biking

Flowchart Key
- Start/End (oval)
- Action/Task (rectangle)
- Decision (diamond)
- Sequence (arrow)

Bryan S. 7/6/95

Flowcharts: Plain & Simple

© 2002 Oriel Incorporated. All Rights Reserved.

SECTION B: DETAILED FLOWCHARTS

Detailed Flowchart: Review

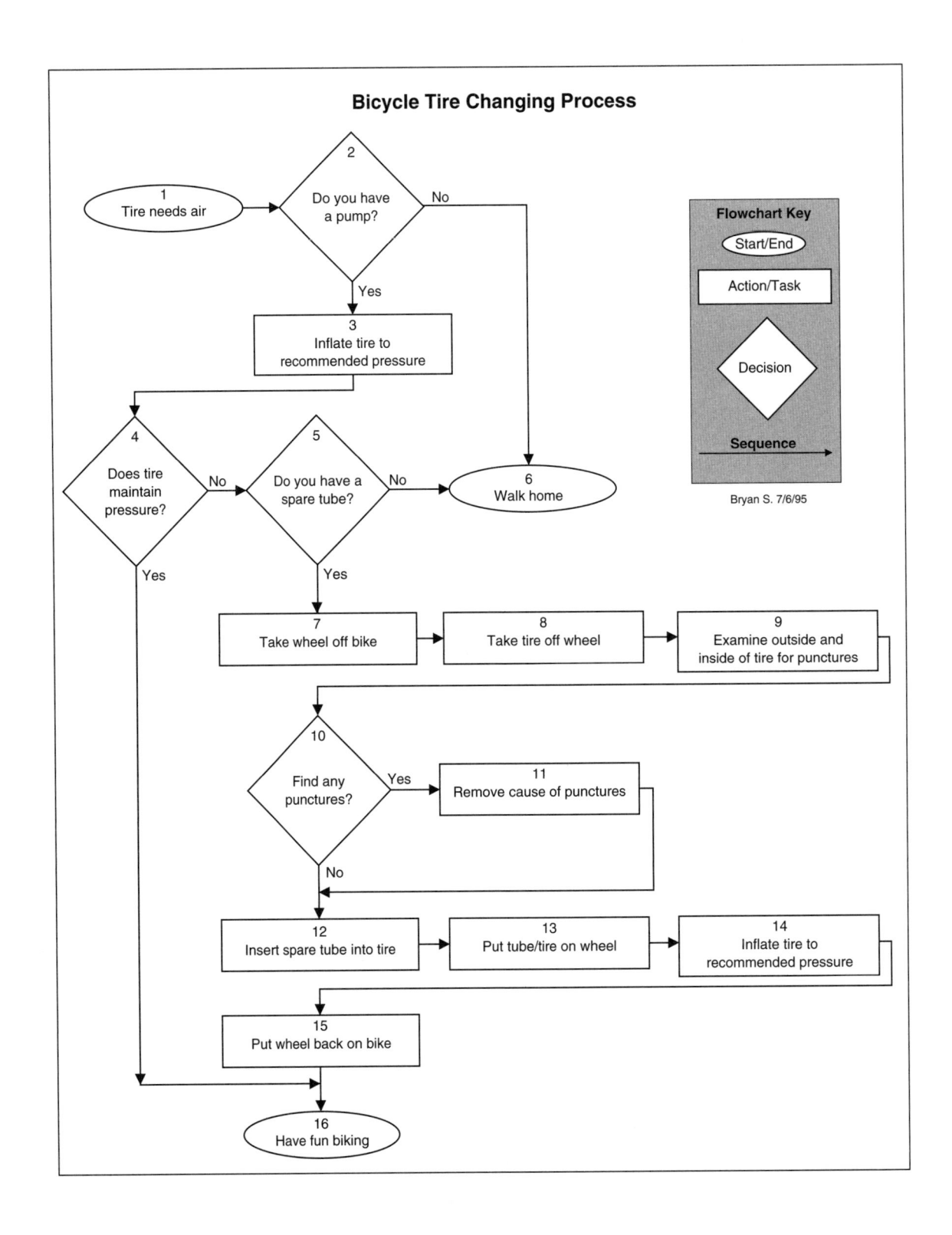

Bicycle Tire Changing Process

1. Tire needs air
2. Do you have a pump? — No → 6. Walk home
   - Yes ↓
3. Inflate tire to recommended pressure
4. Does tire maintain pressure?
   - Yes → 15
   - No → 5
5. Do you have a spare tube?
   - No → 6. Walk home
   - Yes ↓
7. Take wheel off bike
8. Take tire off wheel
9. Examine outside and inside of tire for punctures
10. Find any punctures?
    - Yes → 11. Remove cause of punctures
    - No ↓
12. Insert spare tube into tire
13. Put tube/tire on wheel
14. Inflate tire to recommended pressure
15. Put wheel back on bike
16. Have fun biking

Flowchart Key
- Start/End (oval)
- Action/Task (rectangle)
- Decision (diamond)
- Sequence (arrow)

Bryan S. 7/6/95

38   **Flowcharts: Plain & Simple**

© 2002 Oriel Incorporated. All Rights Reserved.

SECTION B: DETAILED FLOWCHARTS

Reading a Detailed Flowchart: Answers

1. Which are the start and end points?

    The start point is Step 1, "Tire needs air." It is in an oval.

    There are two end points. They are both in ovals.

    – In Step 6 the process ends early when you walk home

    – In Step 16 the process ends with a fixed tire and you have fun biking

2. Which steps are action steps?

    The action steps are the steps in rectangles. They are Steps 3, 7, 8, 9, 11, 12, 13, 14, and 15.

3. Which steps are decisions?

    The decision steps are the steps in diamonds. They are Steps 2, 4, 5, and 10.

4. Step 2 asks, "Do you have a pump?"

    a) If you do not have a pump, what step comes next?

    If you answer No to the question the arrow goes to Step 6, "Walk home."

    (This is one of the possible end points.)

    b) If you do have a pump, what step comes next?

    If you answer Yes to the question the arrow goes to Step 3, "Inflate tire to recommended pressure."

    (This leads to the next decision.)

Flowcharts: Plain & Simple

SECTION B: DETAILED FLOWCHARTS

The Right Amount of Detail: Background Information

As indicated in Section A, a common problem with flowcharts is getting the right amount of detail.

For example, suppose you are flowcharting the process of backing a car out of a driveway so you can teach a new driver how to do this task. One level of detail might be

- Get in the car
- Start the car
- Visually check behind and on both sides of the car
- Put the car in reverse
- Slowly back up

Another level of detail is

- Put your hand in your pocket
- Take out the car key
- Put the key in the car door
- Turn the key to the right
- Open the door
- Sit down
- Close the door
- Adjust the mirrors
- Put on the seat belt
- Etc.

The amount of detail in the second example is probably more than is necessary. Most people using this process can arrive at a successful outcome using the first description. The key is to add only as much detail as is needed to achieve the purpose.

Often, people begin constructing flowcharts with too much detail. If you are unsure what level of detail will be most helpful to you, start with less detail in the first draft of the flowchart. You can always add more detail later if it is needed.

Detailed Flowcharts: Uses and Limitations

Uses

Detailed flowcharts help in understanding, improving, and standardizing a process.

- Diagramming the sequence and relationship of steps in detail can help identify places where people are doing important parts of a process differently. Agreeing on one set of steps can help eliminate inefficiency and errors.
- Including decision points allows people to see when they have to make decisions about which path to follow, and what happens on each path. Decision points are places where problems often occur.
- Including steps taken when things go wrong can expose potential improvement areas.

Limitations

Users can get bogged down in more detail than is useful for the task.

- Documenting detail takes time
- Do not provide more detail than is needed

Exercise 2: Interpreting Detailed Flowcharts

Hotel Flowchart

The flowchart on the next page was created by hotel staff who wanted to improve the process for guests who choose to check out at the front desk rather than use the express check-out option. They want to know if the flowchart suggests any potential process problems. (In contrast to the flowchart on page 19, this version presents the customer's view of the process.)

Instructions

1. Read through the steps in the flowchart on the facing page.
2. Circle or highlight steps that might indicate problems in the check-out process.

EXERCISE 2: INTERPRETING DETAILED FLOWCHARTS

Potential Process Problems

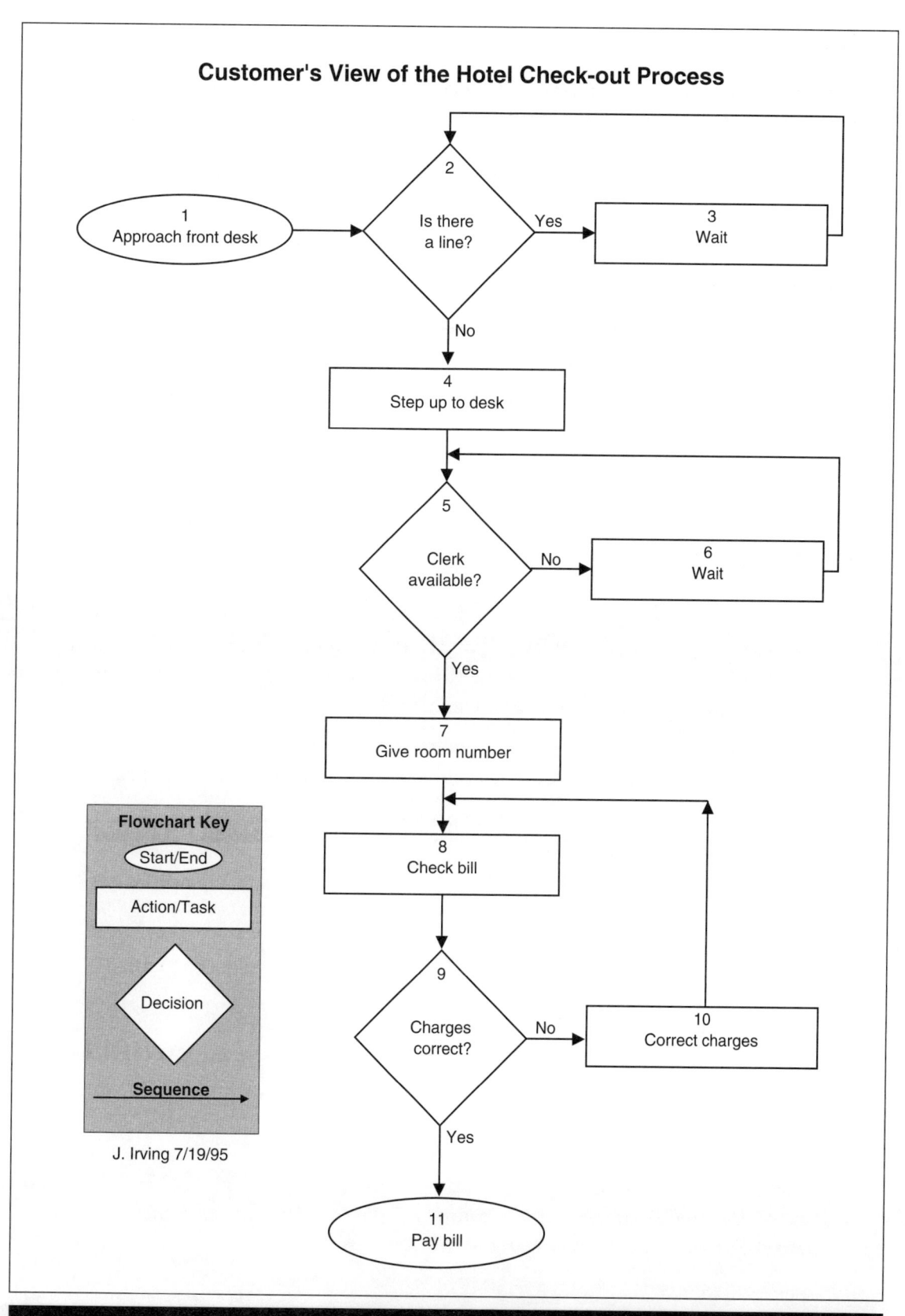

Customer's View of the Hotel Check-out Process

1. Approach front desk
2. Is there a line?
   - Yes → 3. Wait → (back to 2)
   - No → 4. Step up to desk
5. Clerk available?
   - No → 6. Wait → (back to 5)
   - Yes → 7. Give room number
8. Check bill
9. Charges correct?
   - No → 10. Correct charges → (back to 8)
   - Yes → 11. Pay bill

Flowchart Key
- Start/End
- Action/Task
- Decision
- Sequence →

J. Irving 7/19/95

Flowcharts: Plain & Simple 43

© 2002 Oriel Incorporated. All Rights Reserved.

EXERCISE 2: INTERPRETING DETAILED FLOWCHARTS

Process Problems: Answers

Comments on the Hotel Flowchart

The flowchart of the hotel check-out process includes three sets of steps that could be problems for customers. These steps are shaded in the flowchart on the next page.

Steps 2 and 5 show customers checking for problems, which can lead to delays in service (Steps 3 and 6). These steps do not add value to customers and are likely to be perceived as hassles. The staff should collect data to understand better what happens at these points. How many customers wait, for how long, and during what time periods of which days? Data will establish the importance of the problem and will help the staff understand the nature of the problem more clearly.

Similarly, Steps 9 and 10 suggest that errors in a preceding process could cause delays in the check-out process. Data could be collected at Step 9 to discover what kinds of errors occur, on which types of accounts, and during which time periods. It is important to verify a process problem with data.

Improving the Process

Remember that simply creating a flowchart is not enough to bring about improvement.

- To capture process problems, flowcharts have to capture the process as it actually works, not as someone thinks it works. It is a good idea to observe the process to confirm that the flowchart reflects current practice.

- Process problems identified by looking at flowcharts are only *potential* problems. Go to the workplace and confirm that the problems exist.

- Many tools can help you collect and analyze data on process problems. Checksheets, time plots, and Pareto charts are particularly helpful in providing a clear picture of the nature and scope of a problem.*

---

* For more information on tools that can help you investigate process problems, see *Data Collection: Plain & Simple, Time Plots: Plain & Simple, Individuals Charts: Plain & Simple*, and *Pareto Charts: Plain & Simple*.

EXERCISE 2: INTERPRETING DETAILED FLOWCHARTS

Process Problems: Answers

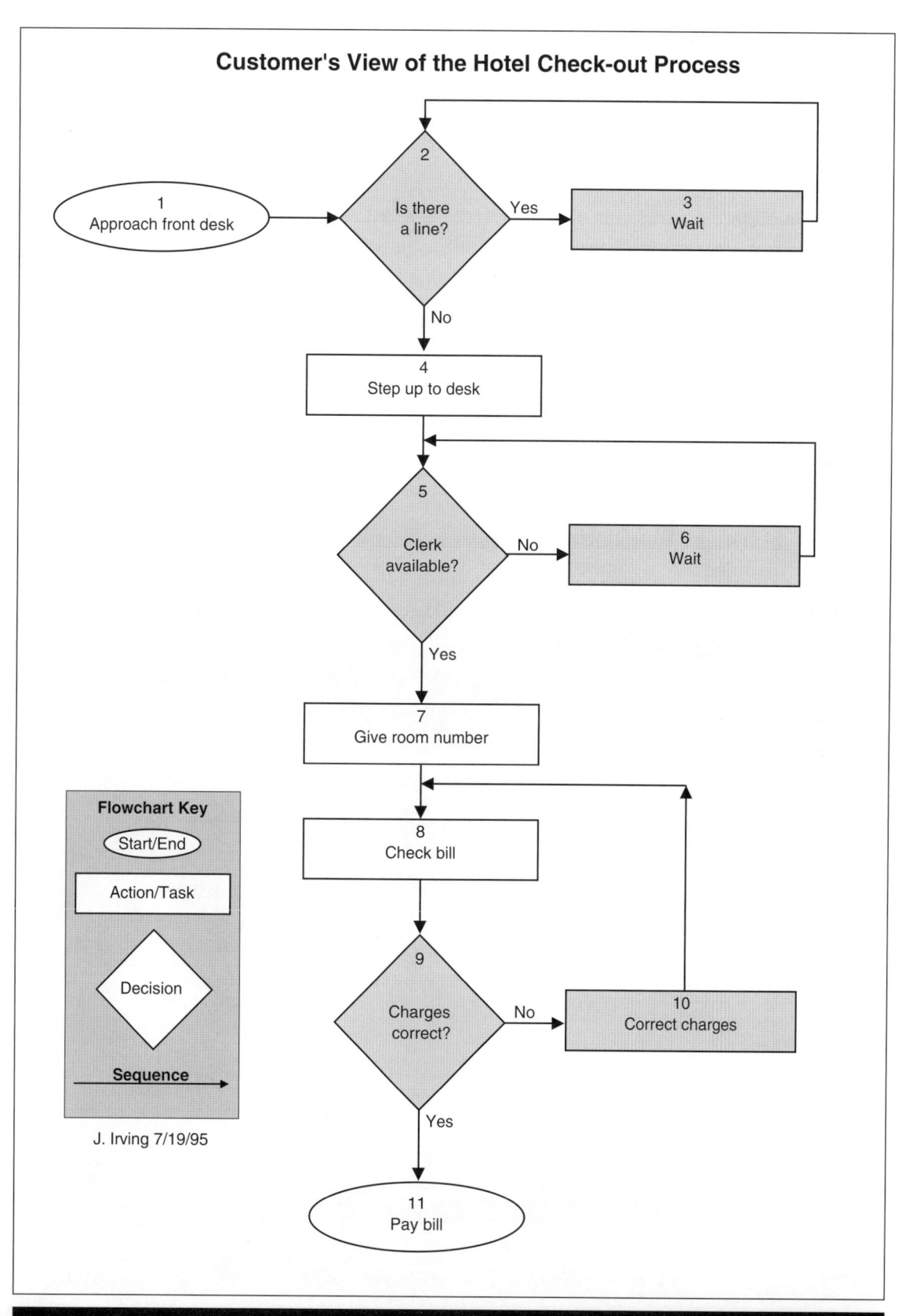

Customer's View of the Hotel Check-out Process

1. Approach front desk
2. Is there a line? — Yes → 3. Wait (loop back to 2)
   - No ↓
4. Step up to desk
5. Clerk available? — No → 6. Wait (loop back to 5)
   - Yes ↓
7. Give room number
8. Check bill
9. Charges correct? — No → 10. Correct charges (loop back to 8)
   - Yes ↓
11. Pay bill

Flowchart Key
- Start/End (oval)
- Action/Task (rectangle)
- Decision (diamond)
- Sequence (arrow)

J. Irving 7/19/95

Flowcharts: Plain & Simple

EXERCISE 2: INTERPRETING DETAILED FLOWCHARTS

SUMMARY: Exercise 2

Key Points About Interpreting Detailed Flowcharts

This exercise showed a flowchart for the check-out process at a hotel. The hotel staff was looking for places in the process that could be problems for guests who chose to check out at the front desk.

The flowchart showed that there were three points where guests might be delayed. At two points people might have to wait either because there was a line at the desk or because a clerk was not available. The third potential problem area was when incorrect charges on the bill have to be corrected.

So far, the hotel staff only know that the flowchart indicates potential problems. They need to collect data to learn if the problems really exist and if the problems are serious enough to require changes to the process.

The main things you should remember from this exercise are

- A detailed flowchart can point out places in the process where there are problems
- Flowcharts have to capture the process as it actually works to help identify process problems
- Data collection can help you confirm that a problem exists and is important enough to improve

SECTION B: DETAILED FLOWCHARTS

When You Can Use a Detailed Flowchart

Your Own Examples

List your own work processes where you could use a detailed flowchart. Remember that a detailed flowchart is most useful when you want to take a deep look at a process that involves mostly one person or one group.

-

-

-

-

SECTION B: DETAILED FLOWCHARTS

Construction Techniques

Techniques for Constructing Detailed Flowcharts

- Use **arrows** on all lines to show clear direction of flow. Arrows, not step numbers, show the flow.

- Use **verbs** to label **task** or **activity** steps. Verbs force you to make it clear exactly what is supposed to happen.

- Use **questions** to label **decision diamonds**. Questions force you to make the decisions clear.

- Include **more than one exit** on **decision diamonds**. Decisions always have two or more possible choices.

- **Label exits** from decision diamonds.

- Use a **bridge** when one **flowline** crosses another. Bridges help avoid confusion by showing where each line flows.

- **Number the steps**. This makes it easier to discuss the flowchart.

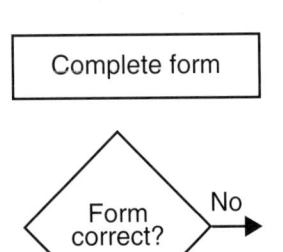

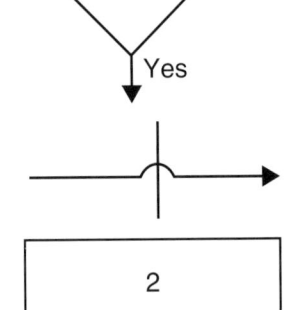

Exam-writing Process: Construction Example

Take a look at how the above techniques are used in the flowchart for writing exams on page 49.

- In Steps 6, 8, and 15, rework loops take you back in the process to redo work or fix errors. In these cases, the sequence of flow is indicated by the direction of the arrows, not by the step numbers.

- The names in the action boxes all include verbs.

- The decision diamonds are all labeled with questions.

- In this case, the decision diamond questions can all be answered either yes or No. The paths are all labeled, and a Yes answer leads to a different sequence of steps than a No answer. (It is not necessary to phrase questions so they have Yes/No answers, but it is necessary to label the paths appropriately.)

- The Yes flowline from Step 15 has a bridge so it is not confused with the flowline it crosses.

- In this flowchart the ovals have Start and End written in them. Some previous flowcharts showed the first and last steps written in these ovals. Either approach is fine.

SECTION B: DETAILED FLOWCHARTS

Construction Example

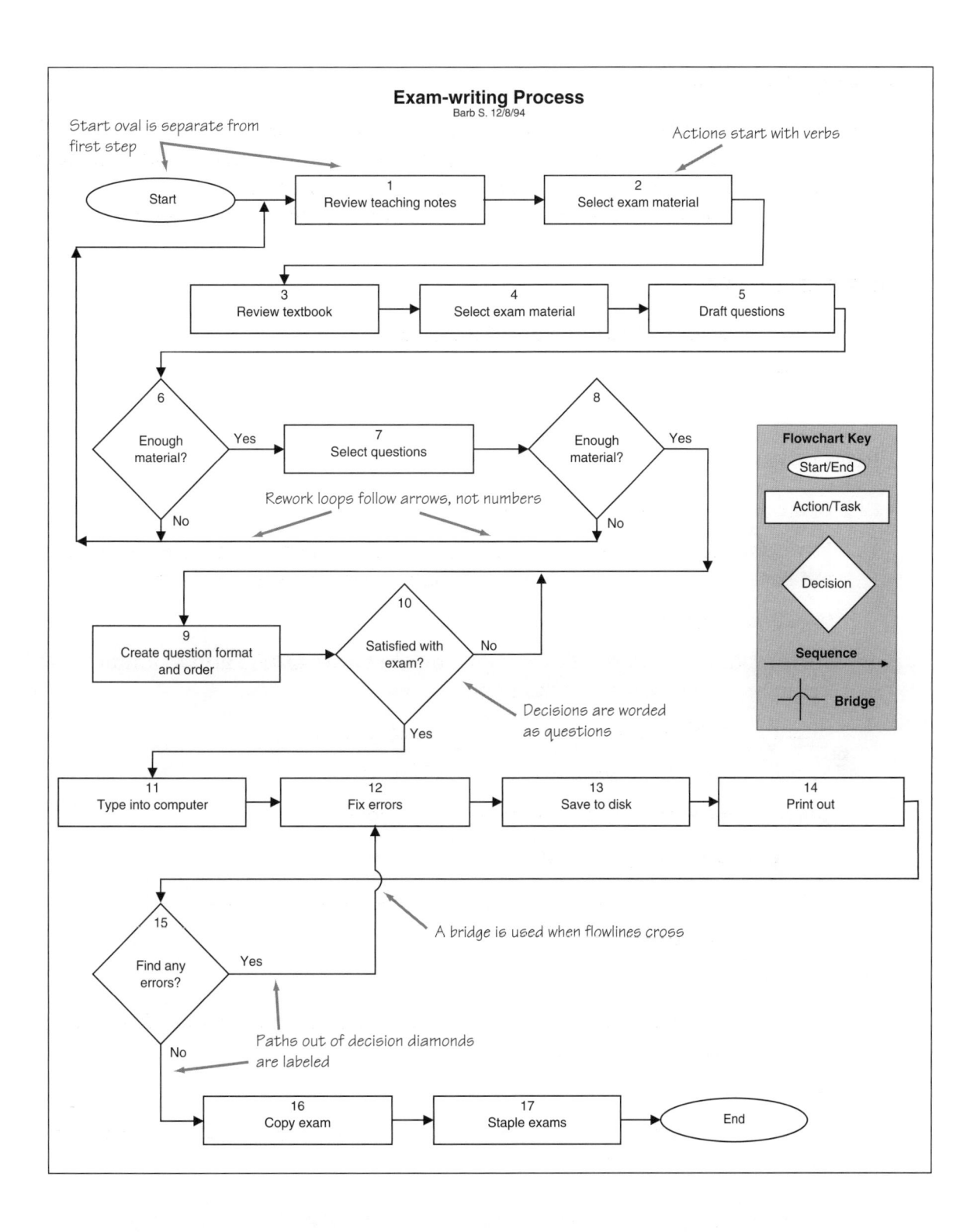

Exam-writing Process
Barb S. 12/8/94

Start oval is separate from first step

Actions start with verbs

Start → 1. Review teaching notes → 2. Select exam material → 3. Review textbook → 4. Select exam material → 5. Draft questions → 6. Enough material?
- Yes → 7. Select questions → 8. Enough material?
  - Yes → (continue)
  - No → (loop back)
- No → (loop back to Start path)

Rework loops follow arrows, not numbers

9. Create question format and order → 10. Satisfied with exam?
- No → (loop back)
- Yes → 11. Type into computer → 12. Fix errors → 13. Save to disk → 14. Print out → 15. Find any errors?
  - Yes → (back to 12. Fix errors)
  - No → 16. Copy exam → 17. Staple exams → End

Decisions are worded as questions

A bridge is used when flowlines cross

Paths out of decision diamonds are labeled

Flowchart Key
- Start/End (oval)
- Action/Task (rectangle)
- Decision (diamond)
- Sequence (arrow)
- Bridge

Flowcharts: Plain & Simple

49

© 2002 Oriel Incorporated. All Rights Reserved.

Exercise 3: Creating a Detailed Flowchart

Changing a Flat Tire

Create a detailed flowchart for how to change a car's flat tire. Assume the car is stopped off the road in a place where it is safe to change the tire. You are creating this flowchart to use to teach a teenager how to change a tire. The steps for construction can also be found in the detailed flowcharts section of the **Flowcharts Quick Reminder**.

Materials Needed

- One **Flowcharts: Plain & Simple Template**
- Small self-stick notes

Instructions

1. Decide on the level of detail needed.
2. Write down all the steps you can think of on self-stick notes. Put one step on each self-stick note. Don't worry about spelling. Don't worry about sequence yet.
3. Decide on the starting and ending steps.
4. Arrange the self-stick notes in sequence on the **Flowcharts: Plain & Simple Template**, top to bottom, left to right.
5. Check for completeness. Feel free to add missing steps.
6. Identify places where there should be decision diamonds.
7. Develop alternative paths out of decision diamonds.
   - Where does each exit point go?
   - If an exit goes back to a previous step, where does it connect?
   - Do you need to add more steps?
8. Add flowlines and arrows.
   - Flowlines usually go *out* the bottom or right side of a symbol and *into* the top or left side of the next symbol
9. Number the steps.
10. Check the final chart using the construction techniques in the **Flowcharts Quick Reminder**. Make corrections as necessary.

The answer to this problem is on page 52.

EXERCISE 3: CREATING A DETAILED FLOWCHART

Creating a Flowchart in a Group

If You Are Working in a Group

A group working together will often create a more complete flowchart than any one person working alone. Having many people contribute their knowledge of the process helps make sure no key steps are overlooked.

However, creating a flowchart as a group makes the process a bit more complex. The steps below can help you avoid confusion and make sure everyone contributes.

1. Clarify the purpose of the flowchart so everyone is working toward the same goal.

2. Agree on the level of detail needed for the purpose.

3. Have everyone individually write down the steps on self-stick notes. Write one step per note. Write large enough and dark enough so everyone can read the steps.

4. Decide on the starting and ending steps.

5. Arrange the steps in sequence on a piece of flipchart paper, top to bottom, left to right. If people have similar steps, cluster them together. (Putting the notes on a flipchart rather than a template makes it easier for the whole group to see all the steps at once.)

6. Review the places where the notes were clustered. For each cluster, select or develop one self-stick note to name the process step.

7. Check for completeness. Add missing steps.

8. Identify places where there should be decision diamonds.

9. Develop alternative paths out of decision diamonds.
    - Where does each exit point go?
    - If an exit goes back to a previous step, where does it connect?
    - Do you need to add more steps?

10. Add flowlines and arrows.
    - Flowlines usually go *out* the bottom or right side of a symbol and *into* the top or left side of the next symbol

11. Number the steps.

12. Check construction with the construction techniques in the **Flowcharts Quick Reminder**. Make corrections as necessary.

EXERCISE 3: CREATING A DETAILED FLOWCHART

Detailed Flowchart: Answers

Here is one way the detailed flowchart could be drawn. Your flowchart will probably be somewhat different. You may have a different level of detail, different start and end points, or some different steps.

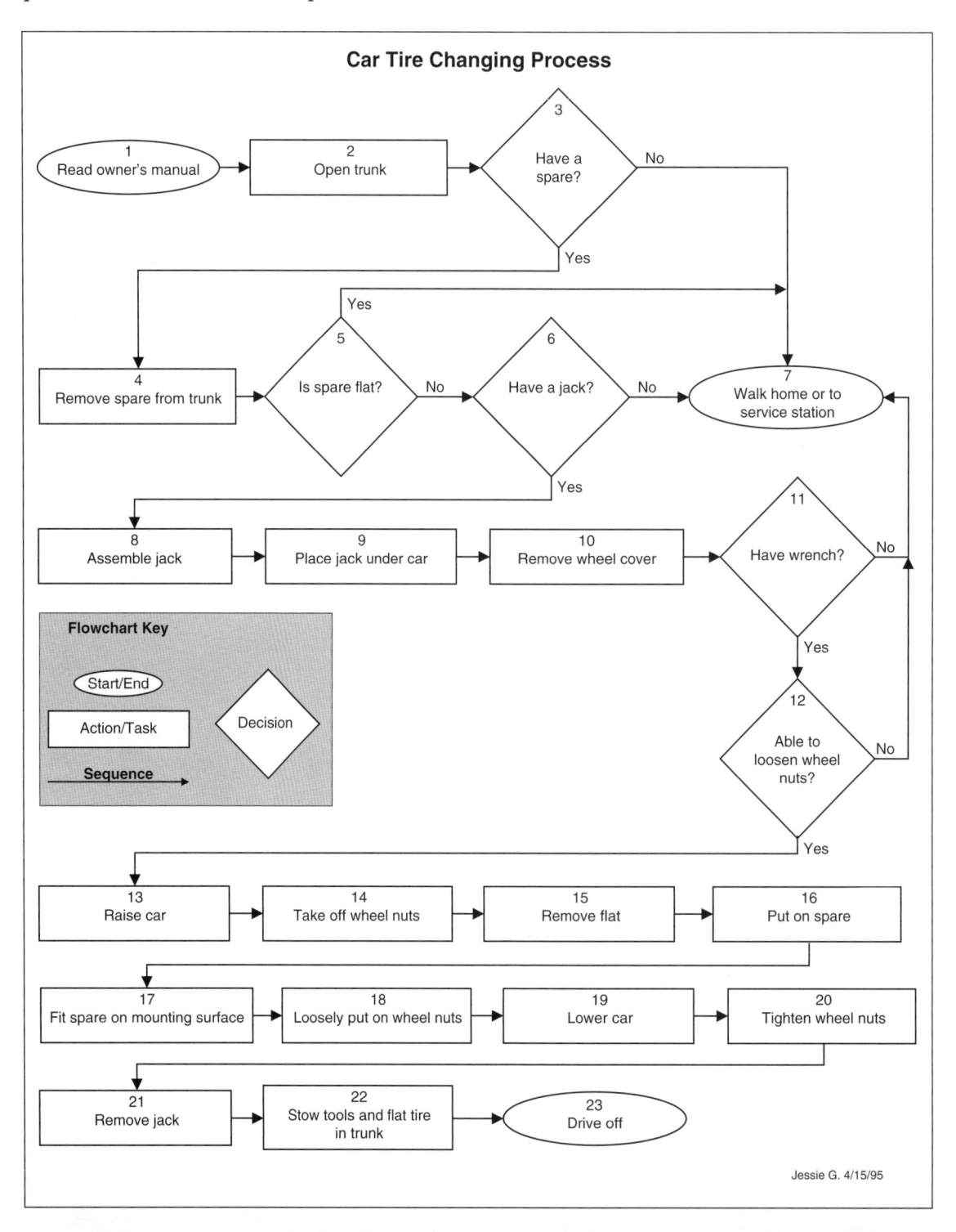

Car Tire Changing Process

1. Read owner's manual
2. Open trunk
3. Have a spare? — No → 7. Walk home or to service station
   - Yes ↓
4. Remove spare from trunk
5. Is spare flat?
   - Yes → 7. Walk home or to service station
   - No → 6. Have a jack?
      - No → 7. Walk home or to service station
      - Yes ↓
8. Assemble jack
9. Place jack under car
10. Remove wheel cover
11. Have wrench?
    - No → 7. Walk home or to service station
    - Yes ↓
12. Able to loosen wheel nuts?
    - No → 7. Walk home or to service station
    - Yes ↓
13. Raise car
14. Take off wheel nuts
15. Remove flat
16. Put on spare
17. Fit spare on mounting surface
18. Loosely put on wheel nuts
19. Lower car
20. Tighten wheel nuts
21. Remove jack
22. Stow tools and flat tire in trunk
23. Drive off

Flowchart Key
- Start/End (oval)
- Action/Task (rectangle)
- Decision (diamond)
- Sequence (arrow)

Jessie G. 4/15/95

Flowcharts: Plain & Simple

© 2002 Oriel Incorporated. All Rights Reserved.

EXERCISE 3: CREATING A DETAILED FLOWCHART

SUMMARY: Exercise 3

Key Points About Creating a Detailed Flowchart

In this exercise you created a detailed flowchart for the process of changing a car's flat tire. Your flowchart probably had some different steps or a different level of detail than the one shown in the answer, but that's alright.

You should still have had a series of action/task boxes along with some decision diamonds. Make sure each of the decision diamonds has at least two paths out of it. Otherwise, you don't need to make a decision. (Notice how Step 3 can go to either Step 4 or Step 7.)

You may also have had more than one ending, depending on whether you had all the equipment you needed to change a tire. It is fine to have "early endings" that occur in the middle of the process. (Notice that Step 7 is an early ending.)

In creating your flowchart, you may have noticed that

- It is not easy to maintain a consistent level of detail
- It is not easy to show the different paths out of decision diamonds
- Steps often need to be moved around as you get clearer about the sequence
- Numbering the steps is sometimes arbitrary when there are decision diamonds, loops, or additional endings

The main things you should remember from this exercise are

- Selecting the start and end points provides boundaries for the flowchart.
- It is easier to follow a flowchart that has a consistent level of detail.
- The flowchart helps make it clear where decisions are made in the process.
- The sequence of steps is shown by the flowlines and arrows, not by the step numbers. The step numbers are important because they make it easier to refer to specific steps when discussing the process.

Section B: Quick Check

Review of Key Questions

Here are the questions listed at the beginning of this section. Check to make sure you can answer them. If you aren't sure about any of the answers, you may want to review this section before you continue.

- What is a detailed flowchart?

- When would I use a detailed flowchart?

- How can I use a detailed flowchart to help identify process problems?

- What are the critical components of a detailed flowchart?

- What steps are needed to create a detailed flowchart?

SECTION C:
Opportunity Flowcharts

This section is designed to help you answer the following questions. Think about the questions as you go through the section. They will be repeated at the end of the section as a quick review.

- What is an opportunity flowchart?

- When would I use an opportunity flowchart?

- How can I use an opportunity flowchart to identify cost-added-only steps in a process?

- What steps are needed to create an opportunity flowchart?

SECTION C: OPPORTUNITY FLOWCHARTS

Opportunity Flowcharts

Definition

An **opportunity flowchart** is a detailed flowchart organized to separate steps taken when things go right from steps taken when things go wrong.

- Steps taken when things go right move down the left side of the page. These are the **value-added** steps.
- Steps taken when things go wrong flow across the right side of the page. These are the **cost-added-only** steps.

The purpose of separating the cost-added-only steps is to help show the opportunities for improvement. If you could collect data to understand the causes of defects at each step and were able to eliminate the causes of defects, you could eliminate the need for both the check steps and the subsequent rework steps.

A review of opportunity flowcharts can be found in the **Flowcharts Quick Reminder**.

Reading an Opportunity Flowchart

Use the flowchart for a production process on the next page to answer the following questions.

1. How would the process flow if there were no problems?

2. Why are decision diamonds 3, 6, 9, and 12 shown as cost-added-only?

SECTION C: OPPORTUNITY FLOWCHARTS

Opportunity Flowchart Example

An opportunity flowchart of a production process might look like the one shown below for a chemical production process. It is not important that you understand the specifics of this process, but here is a brief explanation of some terms used on the chart.

Viscosity: how easily the product flows; how thick or how sticky it is

pH: a measure of acidity

Catalyst: a substance that starts or speeds up a reaction

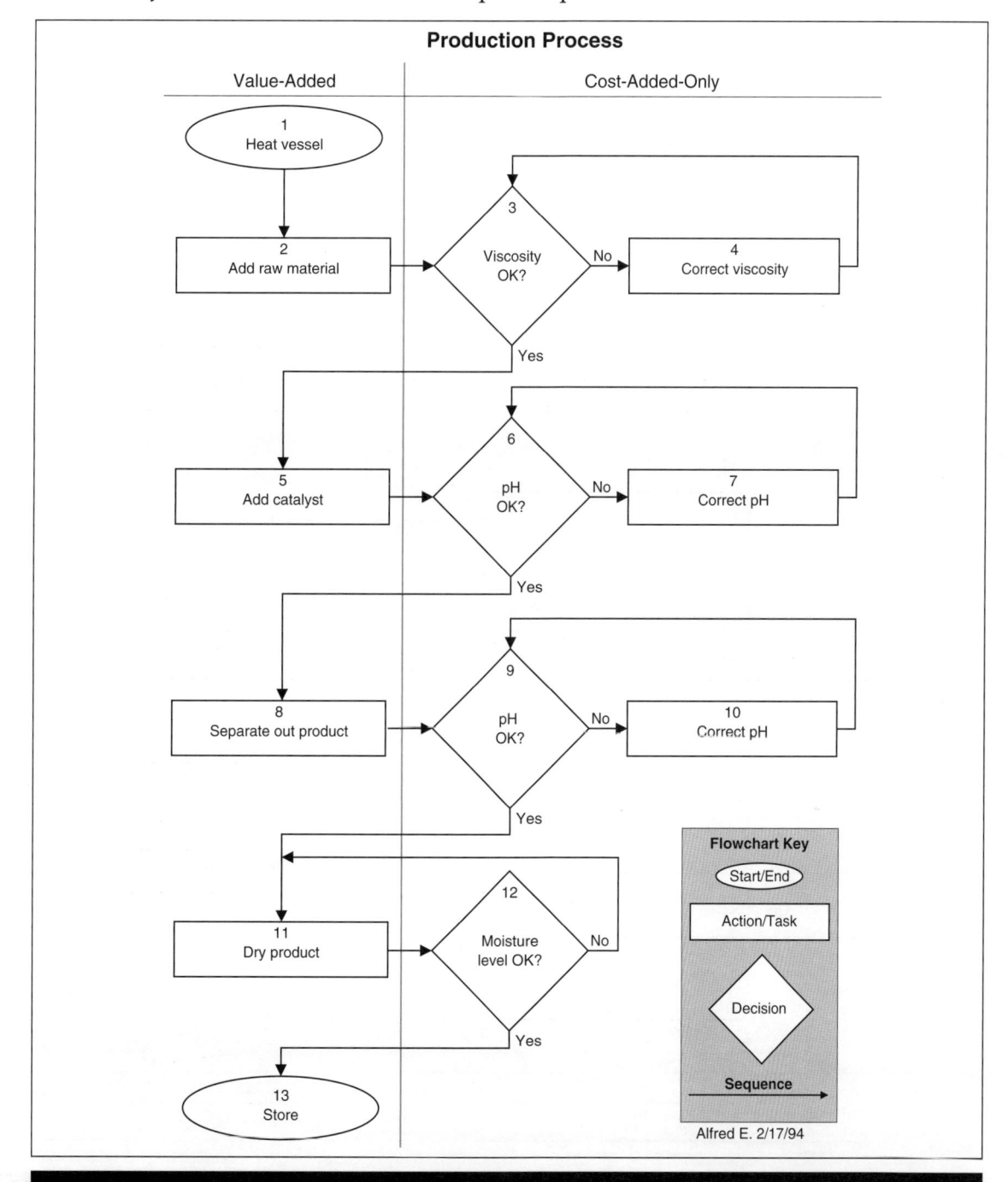

Production Process

Value-Added	Cost-Added-Only

1. Heat vessel
2. Add raw material
3. Viscosity OK? — No → 4. Correct viscosity
   Yes ↓
5. Add catalyst
6. pH OK? — No → 7. Correct pH
   Yes ↓
8. Separate out product
9. pH OK? — No → 10. Correct pH
   Yes ↓
11. Dry product
12. Moisture level OK? — No
    Yes ↓
13. Store

Flowchart Key
- Start/End (oval)
- Action/Task (rectangle)
- Decision (diamond)
- Sequence →

Alfred E. 2/17/94

Flowcharts: Plain & Simple 57

© 2002 Oriel Incorporated. All Rights Reserved.

SECTION C: OPPORTUNITY FLOWCHARTS

Opportunity Flowchart: Review

An opportunity flowchart of a production process might look like this.

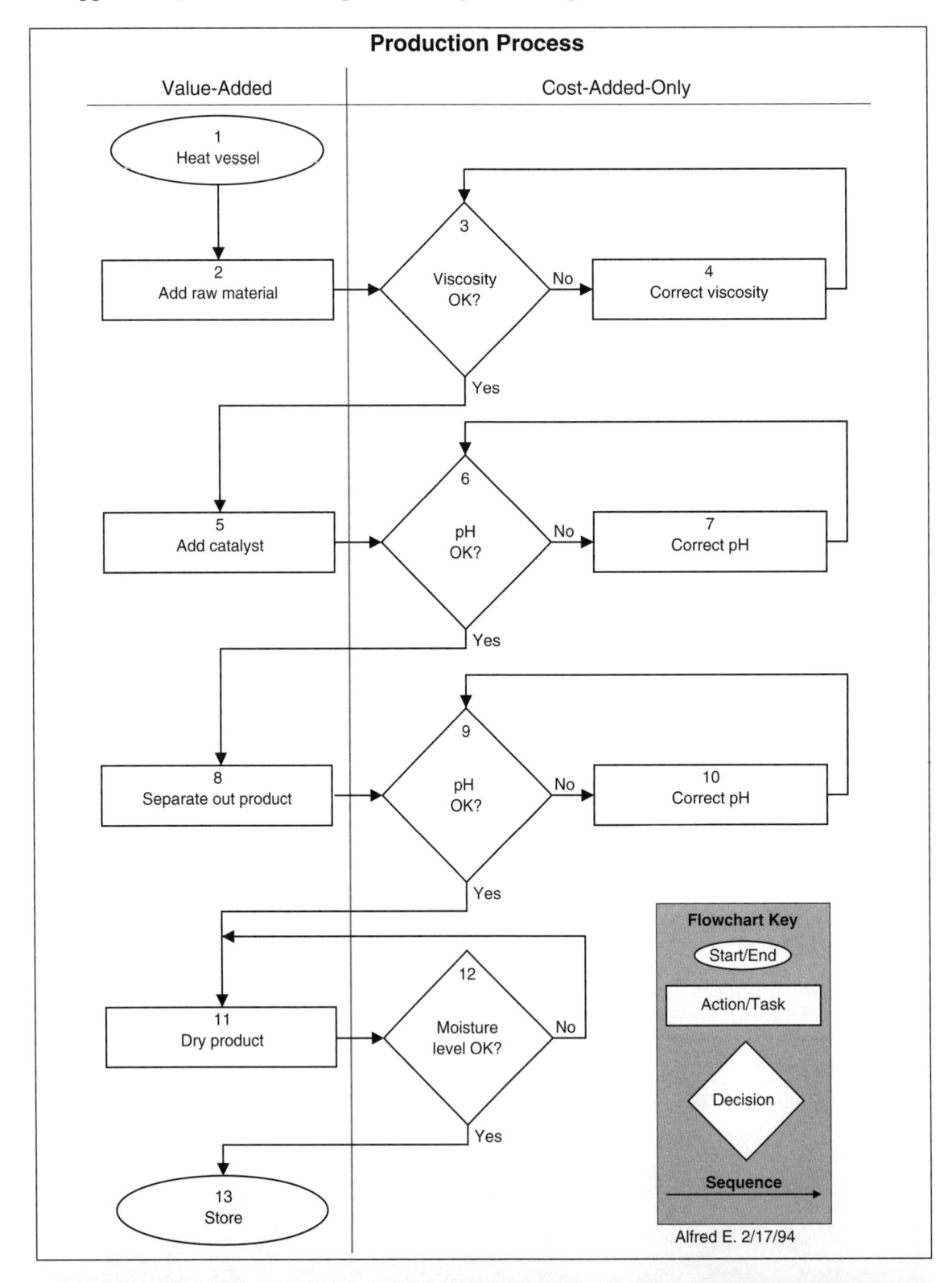

Production Process

Value-Added	Cost-Added-Only

1. Heat vessel
2. Add raw material
3. Viscosity OK?
4. Correct viscosity
5. Add catalyst
6. pH OK?
7. Correct pH
8. Separate out product
9. pH OK?
10. Correct pH
11. Dry product
12. Moisture level OK?
13. Store

Flowchart Key
- Start/End
- Action/Task
- Decision
- Sequence

Alfred E. 2/17/94

Flowcharts: Plain & Simple

© 2002 Oriel Incorporated. All Rights Reserved.

SECTION C: OPPORTUNITY FLOWCHARTS

Reading an Opportunity Flowchart: Answers

Answers for the Production Process Opportunity Flowchart

1. How would the process flow if there were no problems?

    The process would flow from Step 1 to Step 2 to Step 5 to Step 8 to Step 11 to Step 13.

    These are the value-added steps that occur when everything goes correctly. It would not be necessary to go through the rest of the steps.

2. Why are decision diamonds 3, 6, 9, and 12 cost-added-only?

    These steps are decisions that inspect for errors. If everything ran perfectly every time, these steps would not be needed.

    You may have noticed that when the answer to these decision diamonds is Yes, the process continues through the value-added steps. However, when the answer is No, another step has to be added to correct the problem.

SECTION C: OPPORTUNITY FLOWCHARTS

Opportunity Flowcharts: Background Information

What Is an Opportunity Flowchart?

Opportunity flowcharts are a variation of detailed basic flowcharts. They get their name because they highlight opportunities for improvement. Like all flowcharts, they make the process visible. But they take this idea one step further by separating value-added steps (those essential for making the product or service) from cost-added-only steps (those that are included only to check for or fix problems).

Using an Opportunity Flowchart

An opportunity flowchart is created by rearranging a detailed basic flowchart. The steps needed if everything works perfectly should flow down the left side of the chart. Steps that exist because of problems and inefficiencies flow across the right side.

Separating out the cost-added-only steps can help people focus on the problem in situations where the costs of redoing work, scrapping components, or waiting for missing information or parts is a major concern.

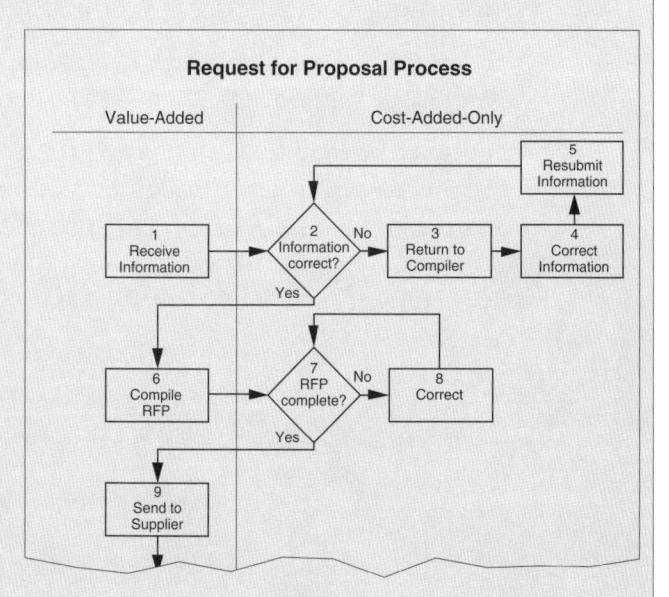

When cost-added-only steps occur frequently it may be important to make sure the value-added steps work right every time.

The Challenges of an Opportunity Flowchart

To create an opportunity flowchart, you begin just as you would for a detailed flowchart—by identifying the process steps. The tricky part is deciding which steps are value-added and which are cost-added-only.

- In many processes, people may think of steps that fix errors as essential and be tempted to call them "value-added." Don't fall into this trap.
- Keep asking yourself what steps would be needed if the process worked perfectly every time.

Flowcharts: Plain & Simple

© 2002 Oriel Incorporated. All Rights Reserved.

…

Opportunity Flowcharts: Uses and Limitations

Uses

Opportunity flowcharts help in understanding and improving a process in which things go wrong. They expose just how much work is caused by errors and missing parts or missing information. Once you've identified steps that are cost-added-only you can begin work to eliminate them.

- Diagramming the sequence and relationship of value-added and cost-added-only steps can reveal opportunities for improvements
- Including decision points can help show which kinds of decisions are part of the value-added process and which are cost-added-only
- Categorizing steps as value-added and cost-added-only makes us aware of inefficiencies we may have accepted as simply "the way this job is done"

Limitations

- Opportunity flowcharts can be difficult to construct
- When steps that deal with problems are not a major concern, it is not helpful to focus attention on them by using an opportunity flowchart

SECTION C: OPPORTUNITY FLOWCHARTS

SECTION C: OPPORTUNITY FLOWCHARTS

Value-Added and Cost-Added-Only

What Is Value-Added?

Value-added steps

- Add value to the product or service
- Are essential for producing the product or service at the current level of technology
- Would be needed if the process ran perfectly every time

Examples of value-added steps:

- Entering an order into the computer
- Welding Part A to Part B
- Writing a proposal
- Asking customers about their needs

What Is Cost-Added-Only?

Cost-added-only steps

- Are not essential for producing the product or service
- Are being carried out because defects, errors, and omissions occur or because we worry that they might occur

Examples of cost-added-only steps:

- Checking for errors or defects
- Reworking material
- Supplying missing information or parts

How to Identify Cost-Added-Only Steps

Ask, "Would this step be needed if the process ran perfectly every time?"

- If the answer is Yes, the step is value-added
- If the answer is No, the step is cost-added-only

SECTION C: OPPORTUNITY FLOWCHARTS

Analyzing an Opportunity Flowchart

Etching Process

The opportunity flowchart on the next page was created by workers who etch circuit boards used inside computers.

Instructions

Look over the flowchart on the next page. Try not to get bogged down in the specifics of this process, especially if you are not familiar with etching or with circuit boards. Focus on the *types* of actions in the right-hand (cost-added-only) column to answer the following question.

Why are the steps on the right side of the page considered cost-added-only? What do they have in common?

SECTION C: OPPORTUNITY FLOWCHARTS

Flowchart Analysis: Etching Process Flowchart

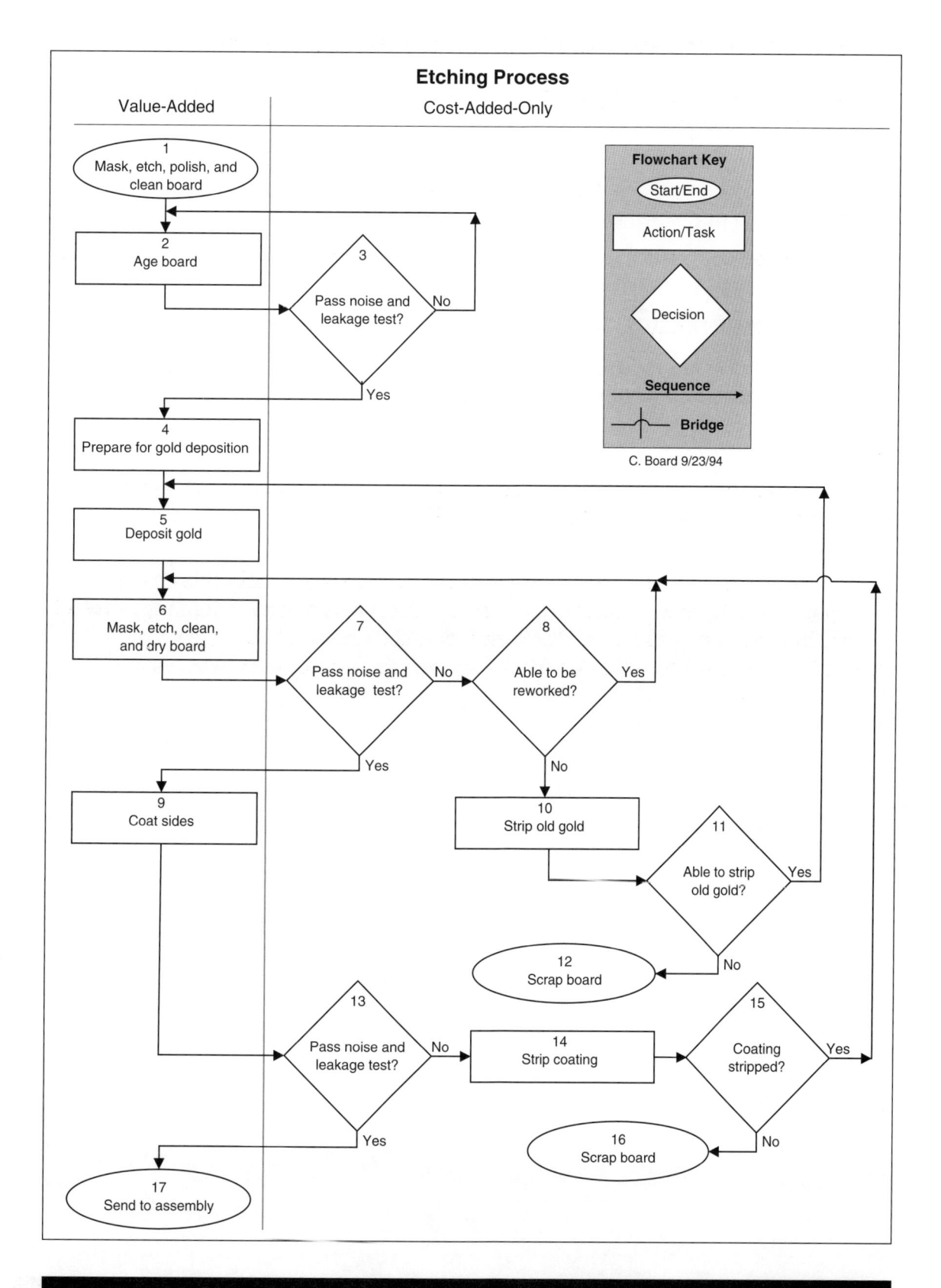

Etching Process

Value-Added	Cost-Added-Only

1. Mask, etch, polish, and clean board
2. Age board
3. Pass noise and leakage test? — No → (back to 1); Yes ↓
4. Prepare for gold deposition
5. Deposit gold
6. Mask, etch, clean, and dry board
7. Pass noise and leakage test? — Yes → 9; No → 8
8. Able to be reworked? — Yes → (back to 6); No → 10
9. Coat sides
10. Strip old gold
11. Able to strip old gold? — Yes → (back to 4); No → 12
12. Scrap board
13. Pass noise and leakage test? — Yes → 17; No → 14
14. Strip coating
15. Coating stripped? — Yes → (back to 6); No → 16
16. Scrap board
17. Send to assembly

Flowchart Key
- Start/End (oval)
- Action/Task (rectangle)
- Decision (diamond)
- Sequence (arrow)
- Bridge

C. Board 9/23/94

Flowcharts: Plain & Simple

65

© 2002 Oriel Incorporated. All Rights Reserved.

SECTION C: OPPORTUNITY FLOWCHARTS

Flowchart Analysis: Answers

Analysis of the Etching Process Opportunity Flowchart

Why are the steps on the right side of the page considered cost-added-only? What do they have in common?

The steps on the right are inspection and rework steps. They indicate that people are worried that the process will produce errors or defects.

- *Steps 3, 7, and 13 are tests of the product designed to sort good product from bad*
- *Steps 8, 10, 11, 12, 14, 15, and 16 deal with defective pieces*
- *Steps 2, 4, 5, 6, and 9 are value-added the first time a board goes through them, but they become cost-added-only if a defective board goes through them a second time for rework*

If the process worked perfectly, the defects would not occur, and the checks and subsequent rework steps would not be needed.

The purpose in labeling the test steps as cost-added-only is to help show the opportunities for improvement. If you could collect data to understand the causes of defects at each step and were able to eliminate the causes of defects, you could eliminate the need for both the check steps and the subsequent rework steps.

SECTION C: OPPORTUNITY FLOWCHARTS

Etching Process Flowchart

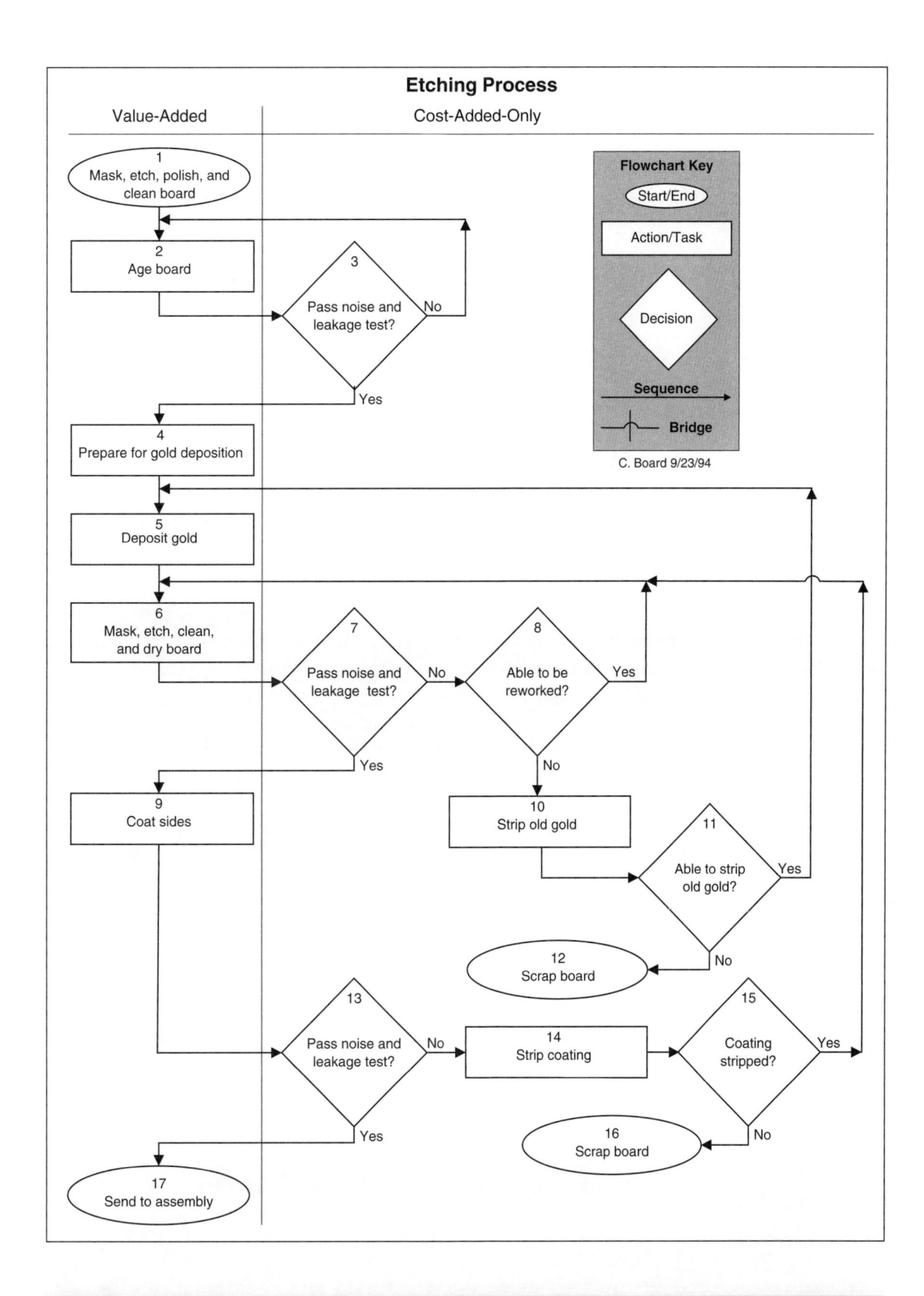

Etching Process

Value-Added | **Cost-Added-Only**

1. Mask, etch, polish, and clean board
2. Age board
3. Pass noise and leakage test?
4. Prepare for gold deposition
5. Deposit gold
6. Mask, etch, clean, and dry board
7. Pass noise and leakage test?
8. Able to be reworked?
9. Coat sides
10. Strip old gold
11. Able to strip old gold?
12. Scrap board
13. Pass noise and leakage test?
14. Strip coating
15. Coating stripped?
16. Scrap board
17. Send to assembly

Flowchart Key
- Start/End
- Action/Task
- Decision
- Sequence
- Bridge

C. Board 9/23/94

Flowcharts: Plain & Simple

© 2002 Oriel Incorporated. All Rights Reserved.

SECTION C: OPPORTUNITY FLOWCHARTS

Grade Reporting Example

The flowchart below was created by a group of administrators and faculty who were trying to understand and improve the process for reporting student grades at the end of each semester.

Read through the flowchart. Make sure you understand why each step is categorized as either value-added or cost-added-only. An explanation of the steps is on page 69.

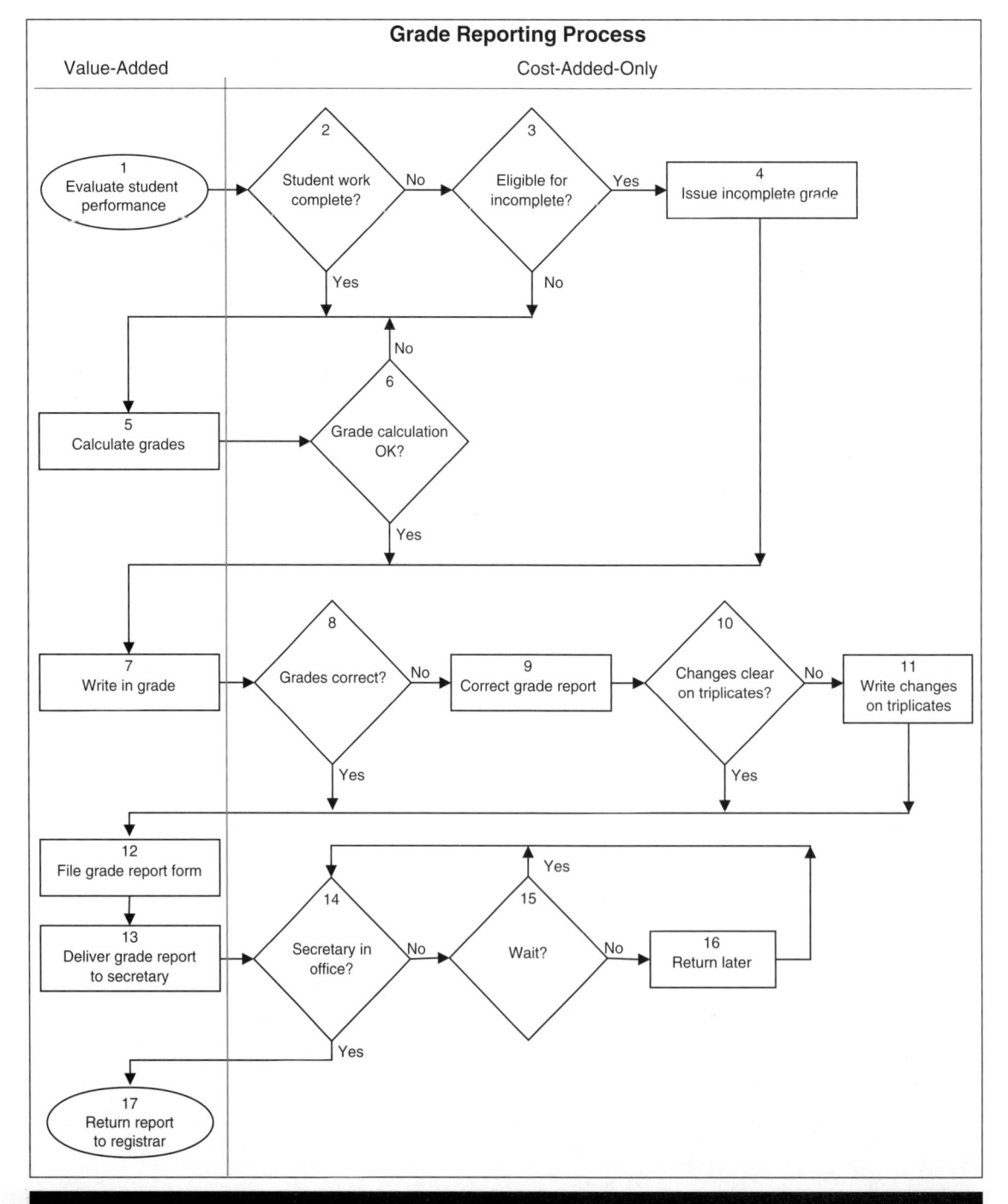

Grade Reporting Process

Value-Added	Cost-Added-Only

1. Evaluate student performance
2. Student work complete?
3. Eligible for incomplete?
4. Issue incomplete grade
5. Calculate grades
6. Grade calculation OK?
7. Write in grade
8. Grades correct?
9. Correct grade report
10. Changes clear on triplicates?
11. Write changes on triplicates
12. File grade report form
13. Deliver grade report to secretary
14. Secretary in office?
15. Wait?
16. Return later
17. Return report to registrar

Flowcharts: Plain & Simple

© 2002 Oriel Incorporated. All Rights Reserved.

SECTION C: OPPORTUNITY FLOWCHARTS

Grade Reporting Example: Answers

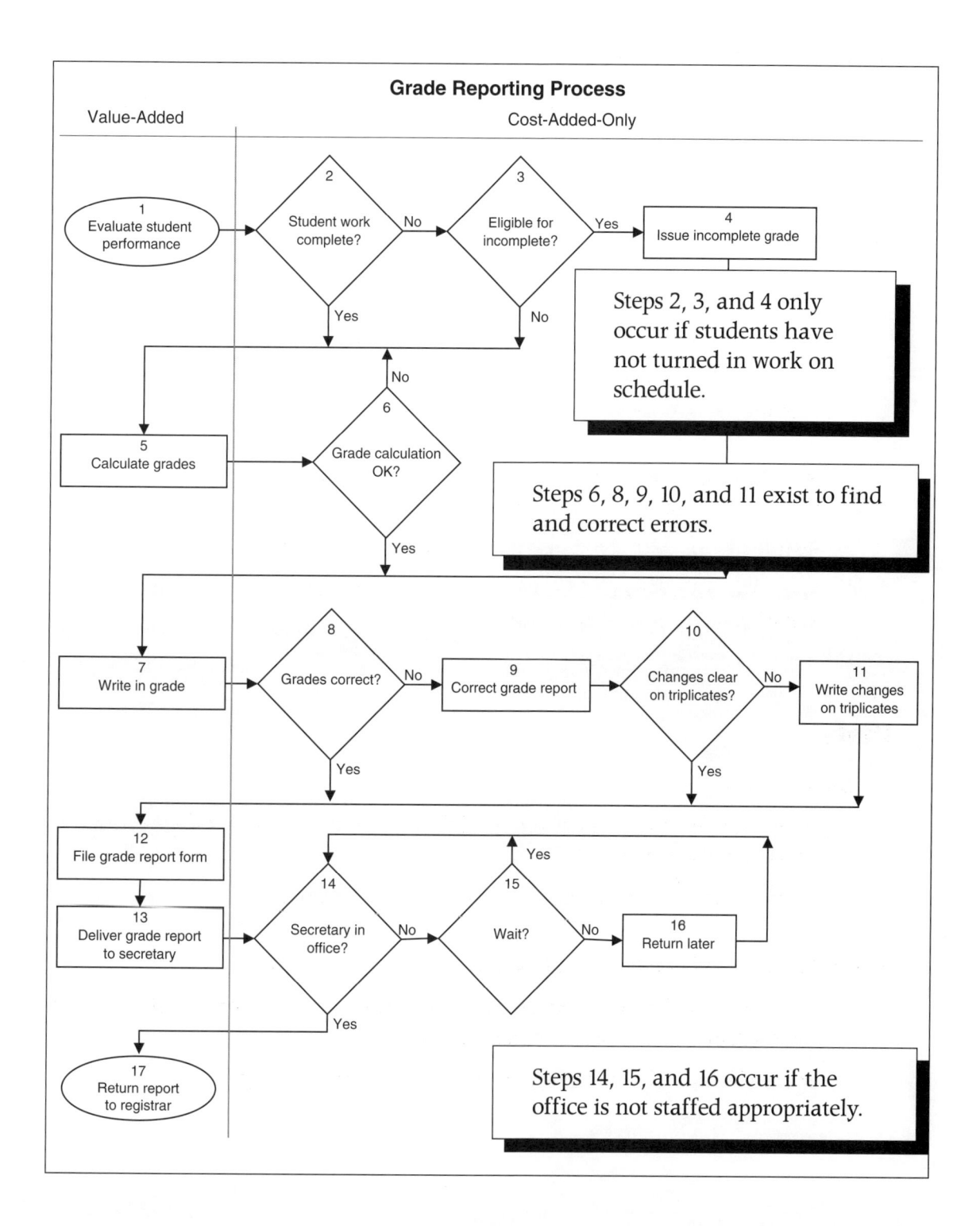

Grade Reporting Process

Value-Added	Cost-Added-Only

1. Evaluate student performance
2. Student work complete? — No → 3. Eligible for incomplete? — Yes → 4. Issue incomplete grade
2. Yes →
3. No →

Steps 2, 3, and 4 only occur if students have not turned in work on schedule.

5. Calculate grades
6. Grade calculation OK? — No (back to 5) / Yes →

Steps 6, 8, 9, 10, and 11 exist to find and correct errors.

7. Write in grade
8. Grades correct? — No → 9. Correct grade report → 10. Changes clear on triplicates? — No → 11. Write changes on triplicates
8. Yes →
10. Yes →

12. File grade report form
13. Deliver grade report to secretary
14. Secretary in office? — No → 15. Wait? — Yes (back to 14) / No → 16. Return later
14. Yes →

17. Return report to registrar

Steps 14, 15, and 16 occur if the office is not staffed appropriately.

Flowcharts: Plain & Simple

Exercise 4: Identifying Cost-Added-Only Steps

Order-filling Process

The next page shows a flowchart for a process used to fill customer orders. Use it to practice identifying cost-added-only steps.

Instructions

1. Look over the flowchart on page 71.
2. Circle or highlight each step you think is a cost-added-only step.
   - Cost-added-only steps are steps that check for or respond to errors, defects, missing parts, or missing information
3. Check the uncircled steps. Does each uncircled step need to occur if everything works perfectly? If not, it could be a cost-added-only step. For example,
   - Step 1 is value-added because it needs to be done every time
   - Steps 2 and 3 are cost-added-only because they occur only when the product is out of stock, or might be out of stock

Hints

For each step ask
  - Is this step here because of errors? defects? missing parts? missing product? missing information?
  - Does this step have to occur if the process runs perfectly?

A decision diamond can be either cost-added-only or value-added.
  - It is cost-added-only if it inspects for problems such as errors or missing items, or is a response to a problem or error
  - It is value-added if it is a legitimate branch of the process

EXERCISE 4: IDENTIFYING COST-ADDED-ONLY STEPS

Cost-Added-Only Steps

The detailed flowchart below was created by a team of people who fill customer orders. Which steps are cost-added-only? Steps 2 and 3 have been circled for you.

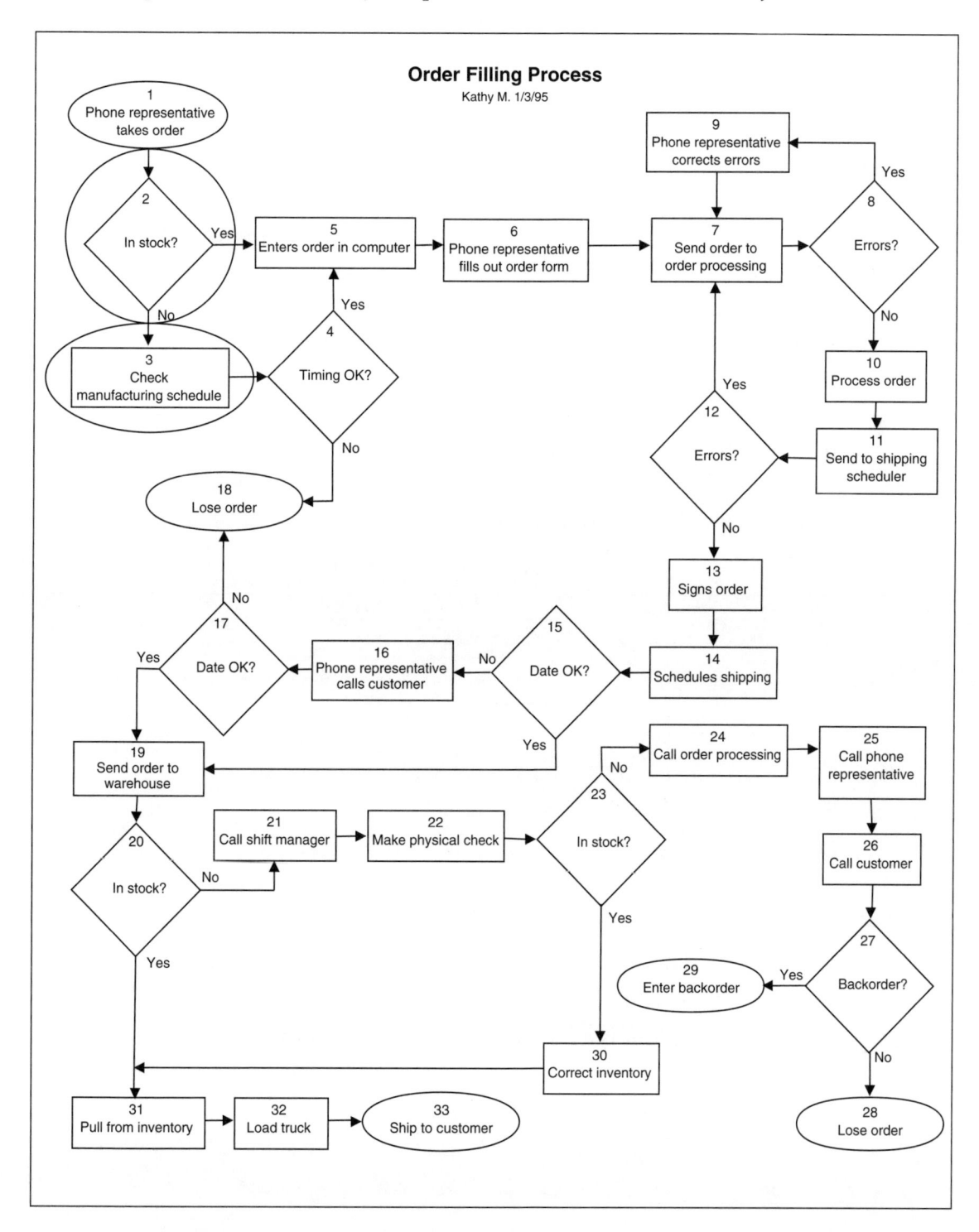

Order Filling Process
Kathy M. 1/3/95

1. Phone representative takes order
2. In stock?
3. Check manufacturing schedule
4. Timing OK?
5. Enters order in computer
6. Phone representative fills out order form
7. Send order to order processing
8. Errors?
9. Phone representative corrects errors
10. Process order
11. Send to shipping scheduler
12. Errors?
13. Signs order
14. Schedules shipping
15. Date OK?
16. Phone representative calls customer
17. Date OK?
18. Lose order
19. Send order to warehouse
20. In stock?
21. Call shift manager
22. Make physical check
23. In stock?
24. Call order processing
25. Call phone representative
26. Call customer
27. Backorder?
28. Lose order
29. Enter backorder
30. Correct inventory
31. Pull from inventory
32. Load truck
33. Ship to customer

Flowcharts: Plain & Simple 71

EXERCISE 4: IDENTIFYING COST-ADDED-ONLY STEPS

Cost-Added-Only Steps: Answers

Value-Added Steps

Value-added steps in the flowchart are Steps 1, 5, 6, 7, 10, 11, 14, 19, 31, 32, and 33. These steps must occur for an order to be filled.

Cost-Added-Only Steps

The remaining steps are cost-added-only.

- Note that Steps 7, 10, and 11 are value-added the first time an order passes through, but become cost-added-only if an order recycles through the steps because of errors.

- Signing the order in Step 13 is an approval step that is in the process only to *catch errors* before scheduling shipping. That means it is cost-added-only.

- The checks in Steps 20 and 23 occur because discrepancies between computer inventory and physical inventory cause errors in Step 2.

The flowchart below shows how an opportunity flowchart could be drawn for the order filling process.

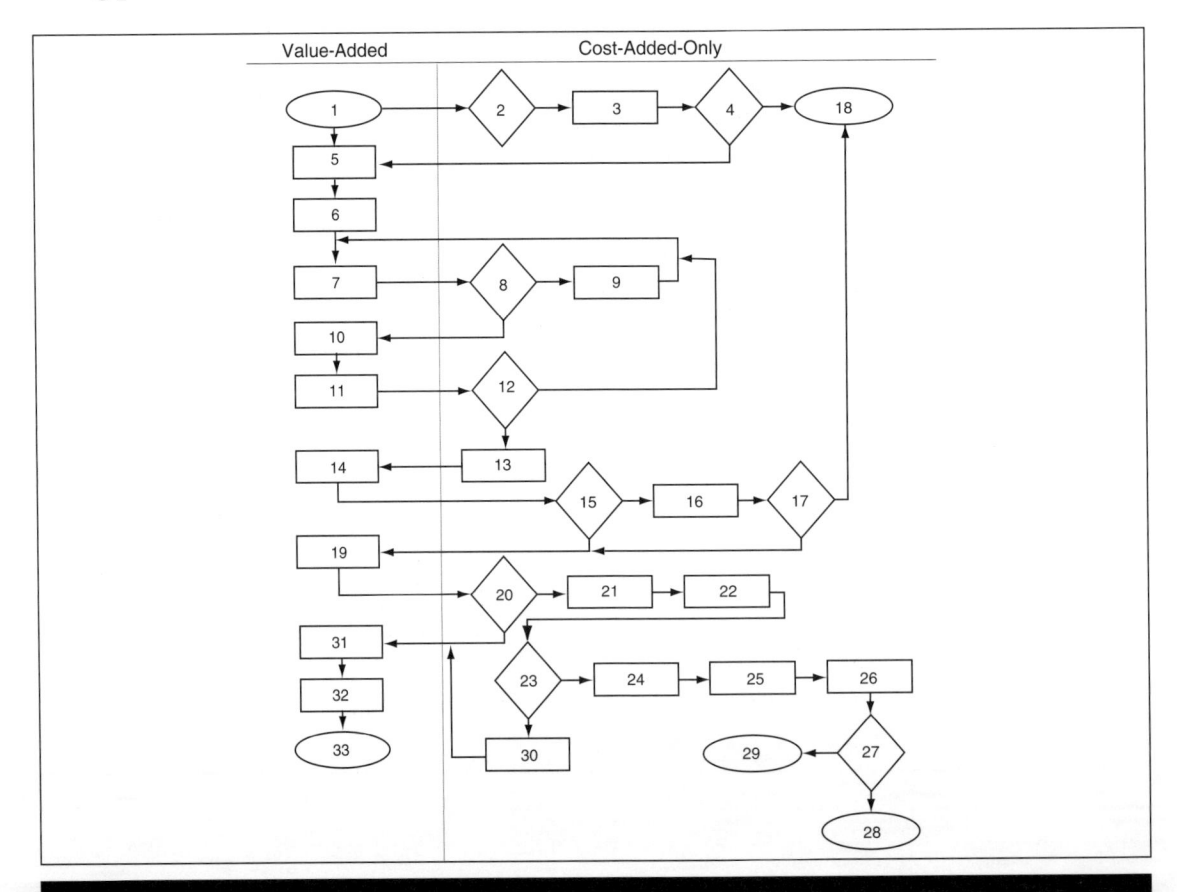

EXERCISE 4: IDENTIFYING COST-ADDED-ONLY STEPS

Cost-Added-Only Steps: Answers

The flowchart below has the cost-added-only steps shaded in. Many steps in the process exist to check for or respond to errors or missing items.

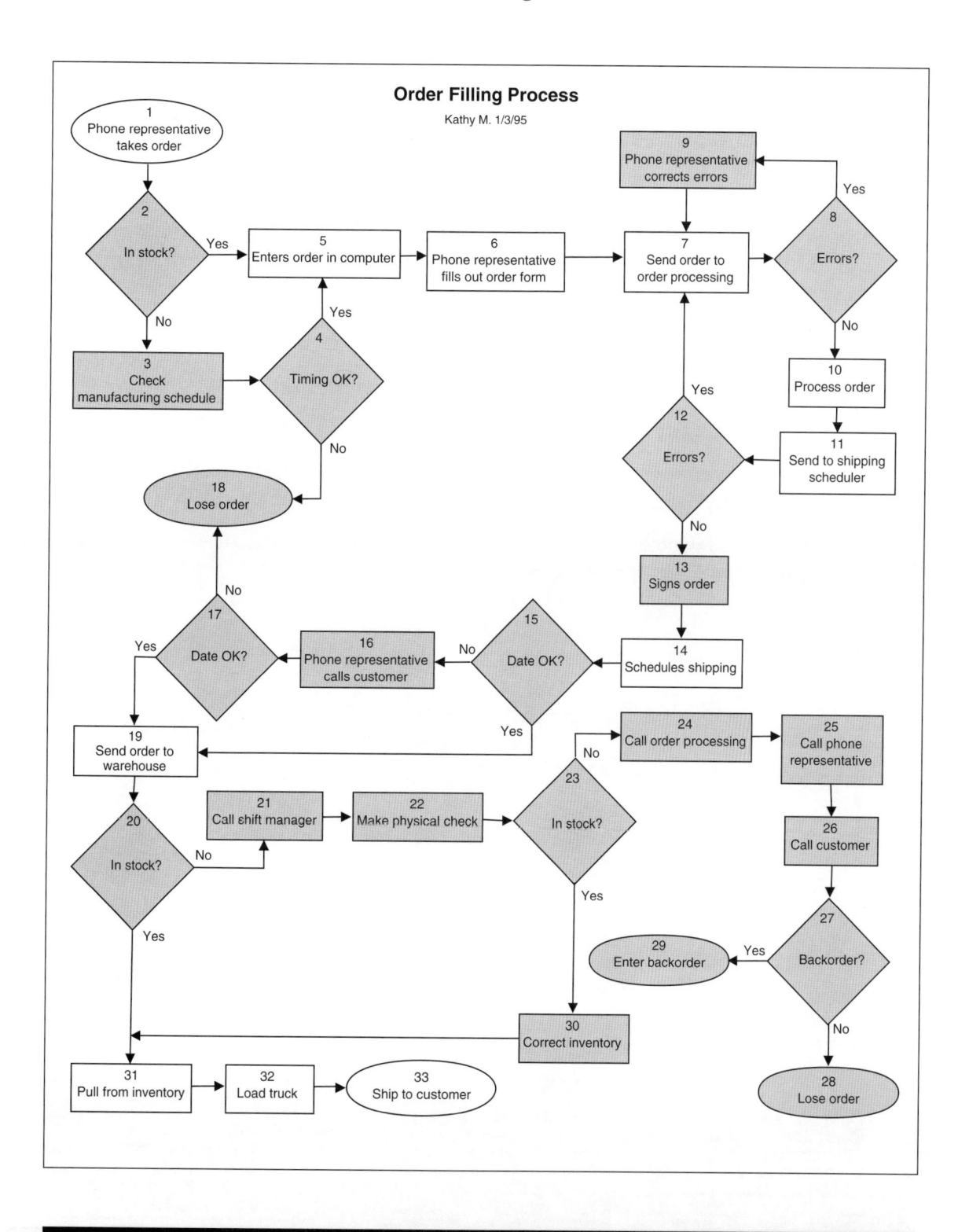

Order Filling Process
Kathy M. 1/3/95

1. Phone representative takes order
2. In stock?
3. Check manufacturing schedule
4. Timing OK?
5. Enters order in computer
6. Phone representative fills out order form
7. Send order to order processing
8. Errors?
9. Phone representative corrects errors
10. Process order
11. Send to shipping scheduler
12. Errors?
13. Signs order
14. Schedules shipping
15. Date OK?
16. Phone representative calls customer
17. Date OK?
18. Lose order
19. Send order to warehouse
20. In stock?
21. Call shift manager
22. Make physical check
23. In stock?
24. Call order processing
25. Call phone representative
26. Call customer
27. Backorder?
28. Lose order
29. Enter backorder
30. Correct inventory
31. Pull from inventory
32. Load truck
33. Ship to customer

Flowcharts: Plain & Simple 73

© 2002 Oriel Incorporated. All Rights Reserved.

EXERCISE 4: IDENTIFYING COST-ADDED-ONLY STEPS

SUMMARY: Exercise 4

Key Points About Identifying Cost-Added-Only Steps

This exercise showed a detailed flowchart for a process used to fill customer orders.

An analysis of the flowchart showed that there are many steps that are cost-added-only. They only need to occur when there is an error or something goes wrong. Otherwise, they do not add value to the process. Many of these steps result in losing the order (Steps 18 and 28).

Of the original 33 steps, only 11 are value-added. These are the steps that always have to occur to fill customer orders. Until we try to create an opportunity flowchart for a process, it is easy to believe that most of the steps we take are necessary. Only through careful analysis do we discover the steps that are cost-added-only.

The main things you should remember from this exercise are

- Cost-added-only steps can be difficult to identify
- In processes where there are many errors or defects, there are often more cost-added-only steps than value-added steps
- When we become used to cost-added-only steps, it is difficult to realize that they don't need to be part of the process

SECTION C: OPPORTUNITY FLOWCHARTS

When You Can Use an Opportunity Flowchart

Your Own Examples

List your own work processes where you could use an opportunity flowchart. Think of processes that have lots of steps for when things go wrong.

-
-
-
-
-

Exercise 5: Creating an Opportunity Flowchart

A Medical Laboratory

A medical laboratory is part of a clinic that is trying to improve patient service by reducing waiting times. The detailed flowchart on the next page shows what happens when the lab staff are preparing to collect blood.

Use the flowchart to create an opportunity flowchart for this process. The steps are listed below and in the opportunity flowcharts section of the **Flowcharts Quick Reminder**.

Materials Needed

- One **Flowcharts: Plain & Simple Template**
- Small self-stick notes

Instructions

1. Look over the detailed flowchart on page 77.
2. Circle each cost-added-only step. A cost-added-only step checks for or responds to errors, defects, missing items, or missing information.
3. Check the uncircled steps. Does each uncircled step need to occur if everything goes right? If not, it could be a cost-added-only step.
4. Copy the flowchart steps onto self-stick notes. Put one step per note.
5. Draw two columns on the template. The right-hand column should be three times wider than the left-hand column.
   - Label the left column Value-Added
   - Label the right column Cost-Added-Only
6. Arrange the steps.
   - Usually the first step goes in the Value-Added column
   - Place each succeeding step onto the appropriate side of the page
   - To decide whether a step is value-added or cost-added-only, ask "Would this step be needed if the process ran perfectly every time?"
7. If necessary, rearrange steps to simplify the chart and make the flow of steps clear.
8. Add flowlines and arrows.
9. Check the construction. Make corrections as necessary.

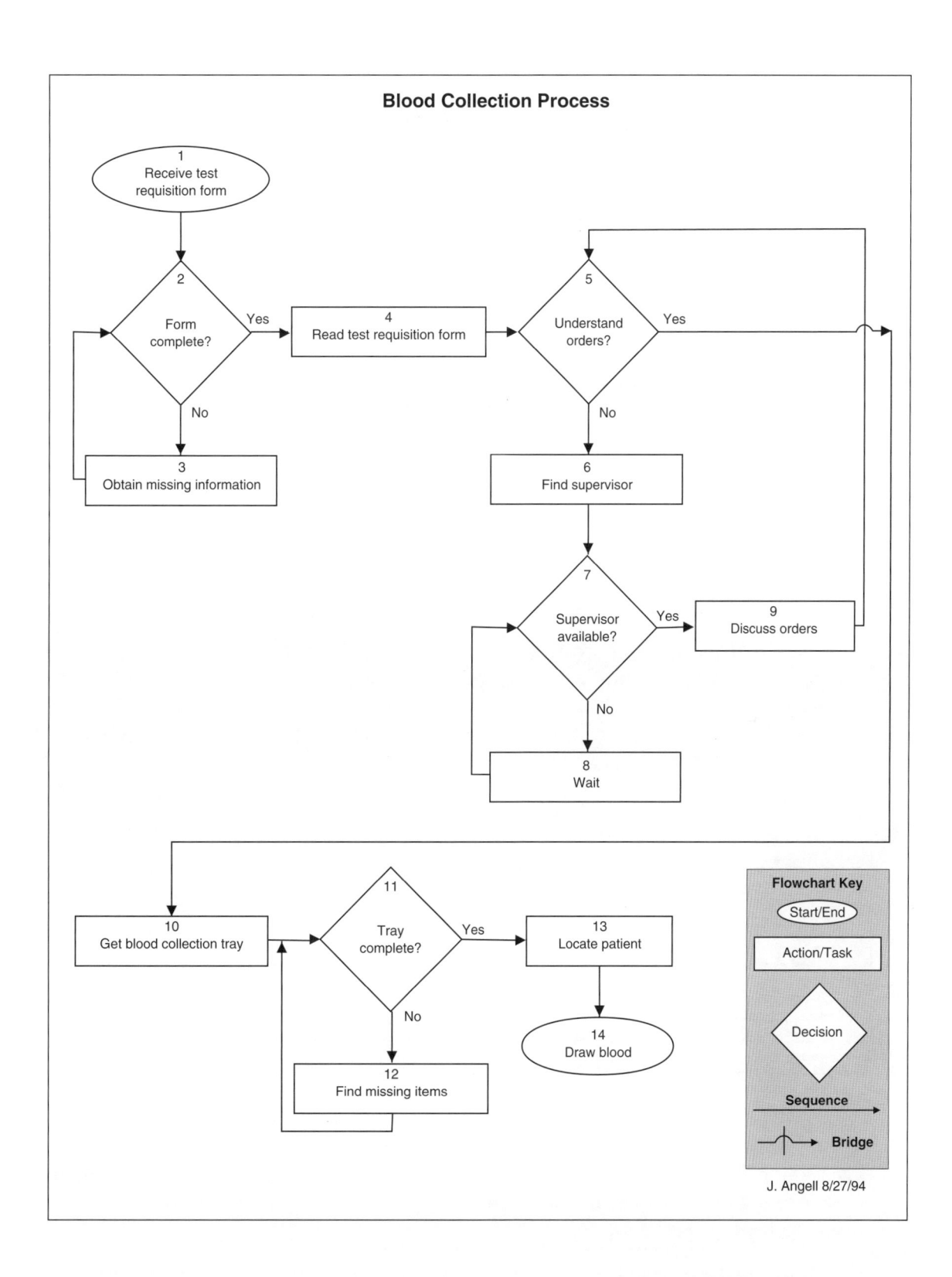

EXERCISE 5: CREATING AN OPPORTUNITY FLOWCHART

Blood Collection Process

Blood Collection Process

1. Receive test requisition form
2. Form complete?
   - No → 3. Obtain missing information → (back to 2)
   - Yes → 4. Read test requisition form
5. Understand orders?
   - Yes → 10
   - No → 6. Find supervisor
7. Supervisor available?
   - Yes → 9. Discuss orders → (back to 5)
   - No → 8. Wait → (back to 7)
10. Get blood collection tray
11. Tray complete?
    - No → 12. Find missing items → (back to 11)
    - Yes → 13. Locate patient
14. Draw blood

Flowchart Key
- Start/End (oval)
- Action/Task (rectangle)
- Decision (diamond)
- Sequence (arrow)
- Bridge

J. Angell 8/27/94

Flowcharts: Plain & Simple

EXERCISE 5: CREATING AN OPPORTUNITY FLOWCHART

Opportunity Flowchart: Answers

Here is one way the opportunity flowchart could be drawn. Your flowchart may look different, but the steps should follow the same sequence.

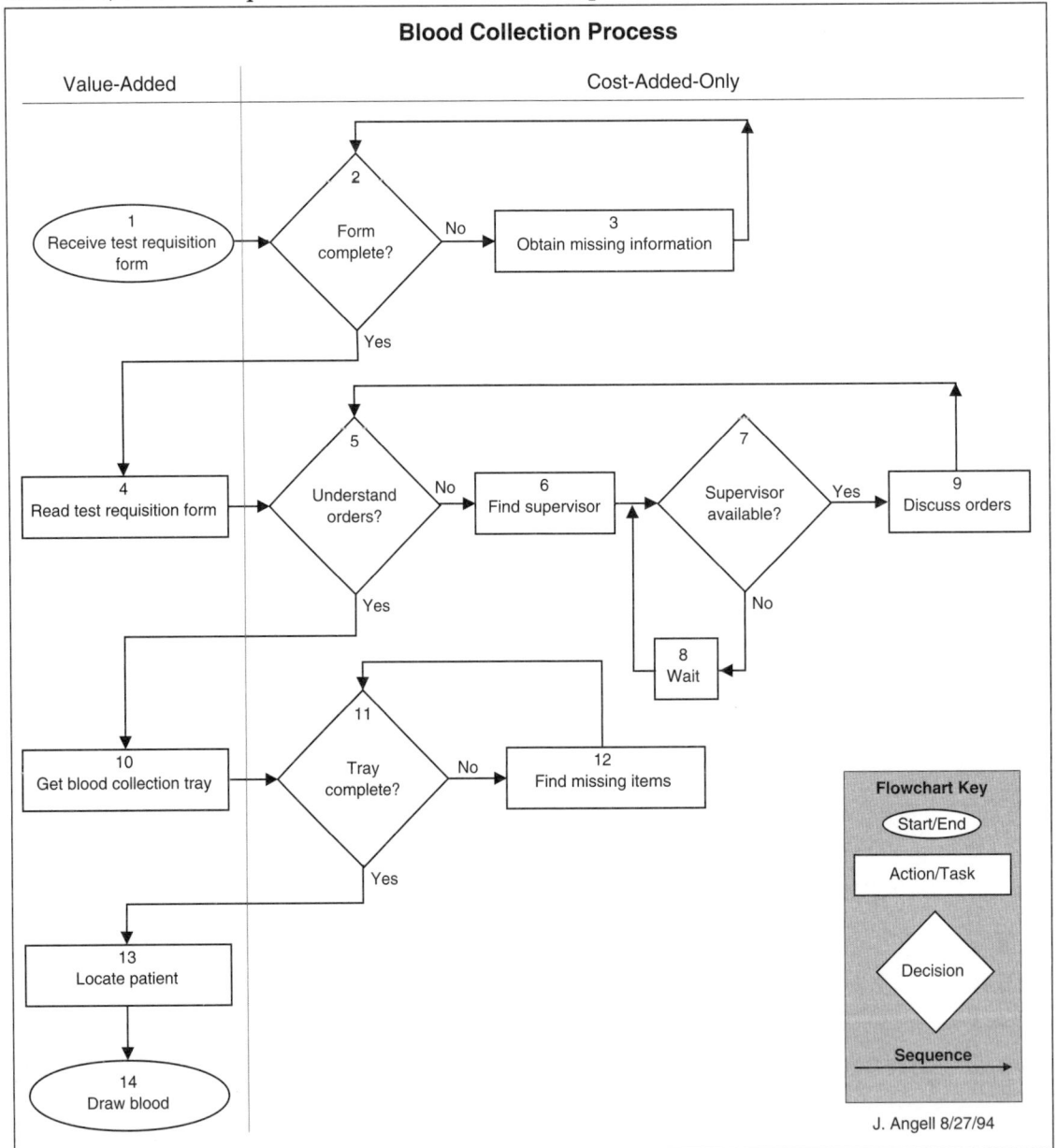

Blood Collection Process

Value-Added	Cost-Added-Only

1. Receive test requisition form
2. Form complete? — No → 3. Obtain missing information (loops back to 2)
   - Yes ↓
4. Read test requisition form
5. Understand orders? — No → 6. Find supervisor → 7. Supervisor available? — Yes → 9. Discuss orders (loops back to 5)
   - No → 8. Wait (loops back to 7)
   - Yes ↓
10. Get blood collection tray
11. Tray complete? — No → 12. Find missing items (loops back to 11)
    - Yes ↓
13. Locate patient
14. Draw blood

Flowchart Key
- Start/End (oval)
- Action/Task (rectangle)
- Decision (diamond)
- Sequence (arrow)

J. Angell 8/27/94

Explanations of Cost-Added-Only Steps

- Steps 5 through 9 are cost-added-only because they would not happen if the process ran correctly. Sometimes you will want to keep an inspection step (like step 5) in the process. It may be cost-added-only, but the cost is small compared to the risk involved if it were gone.

- Steps 2 and 3, and 11 and 12, are cost-added-only because of missing information or items.

Flowcharts: Plain & Simple

© 2002 Oriel Incorporated. All Rights Reserved.

EXERCISE 5: CREATING AN OPPORTUNITY FLOWCHART

SUMMARY: Exercise 5

Key Points About Creating an Opportunity Flowchart

This exercise showed a detailed flowchart for a medical laboratory's blood collection process. Lab personnel believed that patients often wait for blood tests, so they created a detailed flowchart of the process of preparing to collect blood. They noticed that there were several steps in the process to check for problems. They thought it would be helpful to turn their flowchart into an opportunity flowchart to help them decide where to focus their attention.

The opportunity flowchart shows that there are three places where patients may have to wait because of cost-added-only steps.

- If the test requisition form is not complete, lab personnel have to take time to get the missing information
- If lab personnel don't understand the test requisition form, patients wait while personnel find their supervisor and discuss the orders
- If the blood collection tray isn't complete, patients wait while lab personnel find the missing items

By selecting one of these areas to work on, the lab personnel may be able to reduce the amount of time patients have to wait in order to have their blood drawn.

The main things you should remember from this exercise are

- It can be difficult to separate value-added and cost-added-only steps
- Steps often need to be moved around to keep the flow of steps clear
- Even though the detailed flowchart looks different from the opportunity flowchart, the flow from step to step is the same
- It is important to think about the purpose of each step
- The final opportunity flowchart highlights the steps that are really necessary in the process

Flowcharts: Plain & Simple

Section C: Quick Check

Review of Key Questions

Here are the questions listed at the beginning of this section. Check to make sure you can answer them. If you aren't sure about any of the answers, you may want to review this section before you continue.

- What is an opportunity flowchart?

- When would I use an opportunity flowchart?

- How can I use an opportunity flowchart to identify cost-added-only steps in a process?

- What steps are needed to create an opportunity flowchart?

SECTION D:
Deployment Flowcharts

This section is designed to help you answer the following questions. Think about the questions as you go through the section. They will be repeated at the end of the section as a quick review.

- What is a deployment flowchart?

- When would I use a deployment flowchart?

- What kinds of process problems will a deployment flowchart help me see?

- What are the critical components of a deployment flowchart?

- What steps are needed to create a deployment flowchart?

SECTION D: DEPLOYMENT FLOWCHARTS

Deployment Flowcharts

Definition

A **deployment flowchart** shows the detailed steps in a process and who is involved in each step. Each of the people or groups involved in a process is listed across the top of the chart and the steps are arranged in the columns of the people who carry them out.

By showing how work flows from one person or group to another, deployment flowcharts highlight places in the process where work is handed off from one person to another. This is where problems often occur because people don't understand the requirements of the next person or group in the process. They don't understand how their work impacts the work of others.

A review of deployment flowcharts can be found in the **Flowcharts Quick Reminder**.

Reading a Deployment Flowchart

Use the flowchart for a hiring process on the next page to answer the following questions.

1. How many ways can the hiring process end?

2. Who is involved in the meeting to discuss candidates (Step 8)?

3. What do the two assist circles mean in Step 6?

SECTION D: DEPLOYMENT FLOWCHARTS

Deployment Flowchart Example

A deployment flowchart of a hiring process might look like this.

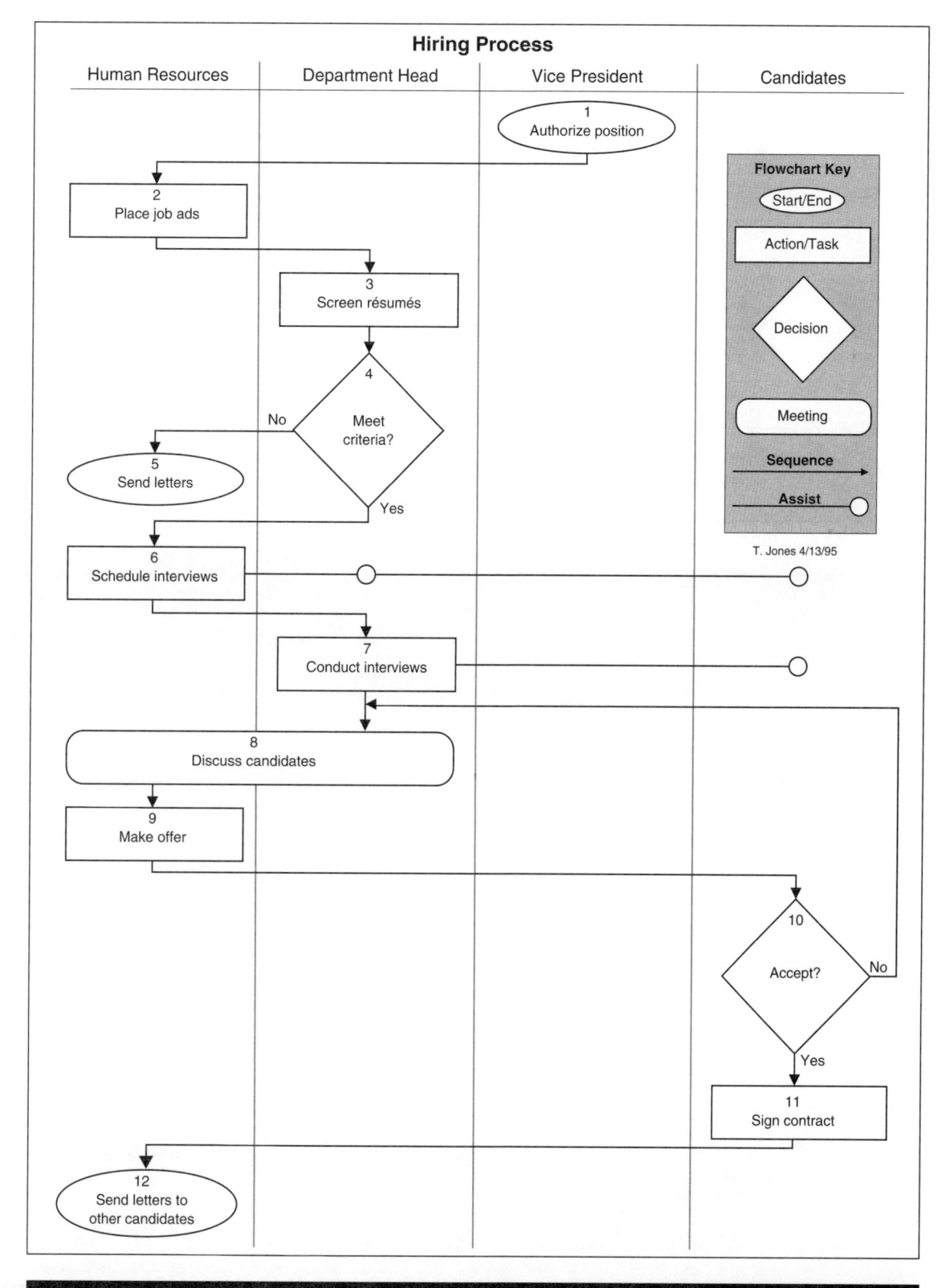

Hiring Process

Human Resources	Department Head	Vice President	Candidates
		1. Authorize position	
2. Place job ads			
	3. Screen résumés		
	4. Meet criteria? (No/Yes)		
5. Send letters			
6. Schedule interviews			
	7. Conduct interviews		
	8. Discuss candidates		
9. Make offer			
			10. Accept? (No/Yes)
			11. Sign contract
12. Send letters to other candidates			

Flowchart Key
- Start/End
- Action/Task
- Decision
- Meeting
- Sequence
- Assist

T. Jones 4/13/95

Flowcharts: Plain & Simple

83

© 2002 Oriel Incorporated. All Rights Reserved.

SECTION D: DEPLOYMENT FLOWCHARTS

Deployment Flowcharts: Review

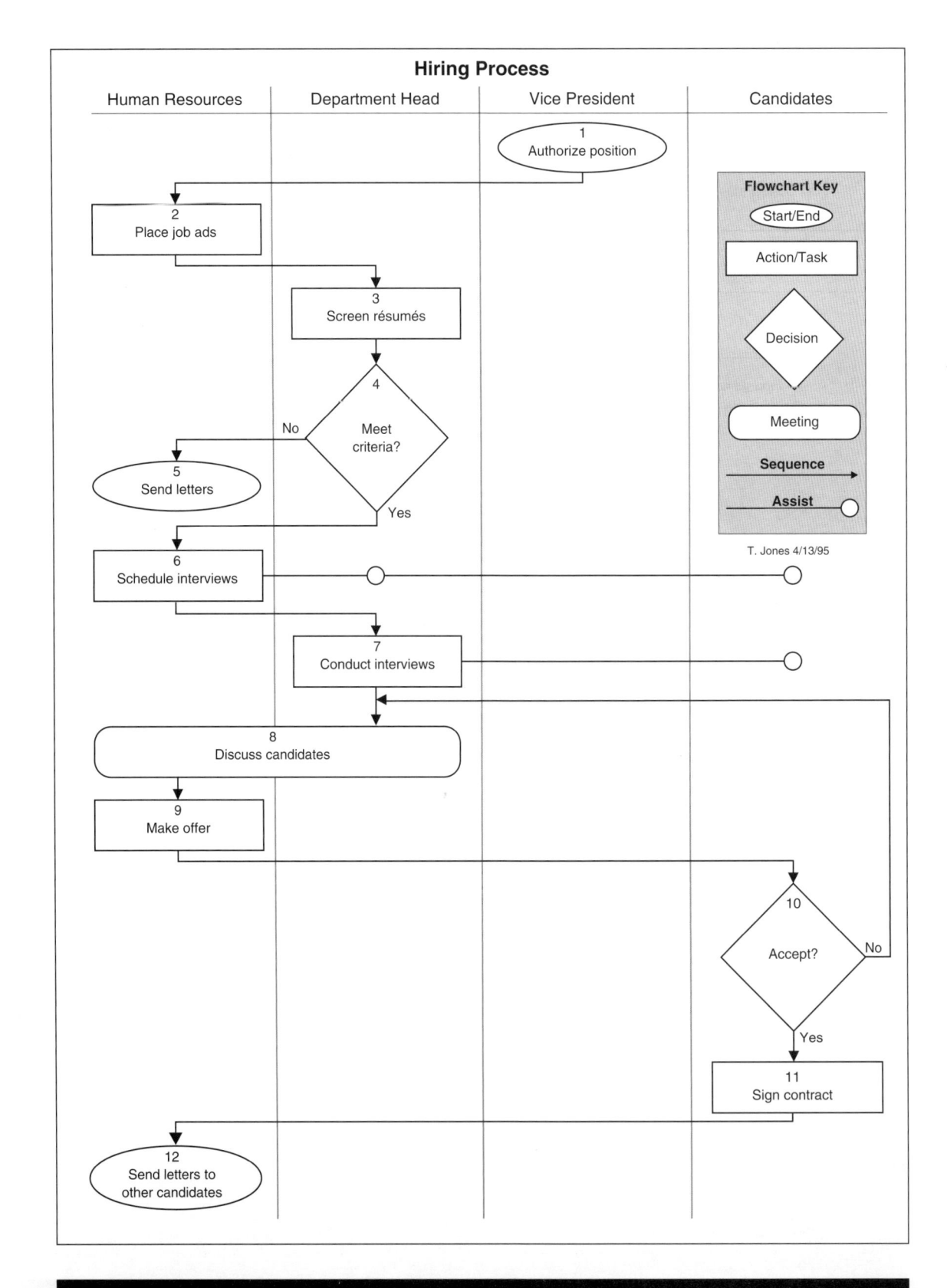

Hiring Process

Human Resources	Department Head	Vice President	Candidates

1. Authorize position
2. Place job ads
3. Screen résumés
4. Meet criteria?
   - No → 5. Send letters
   - Yes → 6. Schedule interviews
7. Conduct interviews
8. Discuss candidates
9. Make offer
10. Accept?
    - No → 12. Send letters to other candidates
    - Yes → 11. Sign contract
12. Send letters to other candidates

Flowchart Key
- Start/End
- Action/Task
- Decision
- Meeting
- Sequence
- Assist

T. Jones 4/13/95

84 — Flowcharts: Plain & Simple

© 2002 Oriel Incorporated. All Rights Reserved.

SECTION D: DEPLOYMENT FLOWCHARTS

Reading a Deployment Flowchart: Answers

Answers

1. How many ways can the hiring process end?

   There are two possible ways for the process to end, represented by the two end ovals.

   - The process can end in Step 5 when none of the résumés meets the screening criteria and letters are sent to candidates
   - The process can end in Step 12 when a new person is hired and letters are sent to the other candidates

2. Who is involved in the meeting to discuss candidates (Step 8)?

   The rounded box in Step 8 crosses two columns. Both Human Resources and the Department Head are involved.

   The rounded box is a symbol for meetings and covers the columns of everyone involved in the meeting. The arrow enters the box in the column of the person who will lead the meeting. The symbol is identified in the key for the hiring process flowchart.

3. What do the two assist circles mean in Step 6?

   The main responsibility for Step 6, "Schedule interviews," is with Human Resources since that is the column the box is in. The two small assist circles indicate that the Department Head and Candidate are also involved in this activity.

SECTION D: DEPLOYMENT FLOWCHARTS

Deployment Flowchart: Background Information

What Is a Deployment Flowchart?

A deployment flowchart combines two key features:

- The sequence of steps in a process
- Who is responsible for each step

This is the only flowchart that clearly shows who does what in what sequence. In a deployment flowchart the people or groups who are involved in the process are listed across the top. (See the example on the right.) The process steps appear in the column under the person or group who carries them out. The sequence of steps flows from the top of the chart to the bottom. Steps that occur at the same time are drawn in parallel with a branched line leading from the previous step into both parallel steps.

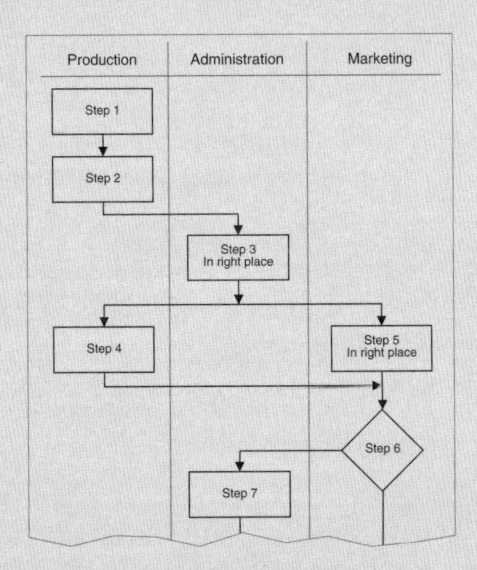

A common mistake is to put the first step in each column at the top of the page instead of placing each step lower on the page than the preceding step. This mistake makes the flowchart very hard to interpret. (Steps 3 and 5 in the sketch above are placed lower than the preceding steps.)

Showing Relationships

This kind of flowchart is particularly helpful in processes with many handoffs, where information or material is passed back and forth among people or groups. Each time a flowline crosses from one column to another, that is a handoff. In crossing between columns, the flowline also depicts a customer-supplier relationship: one person or group is supplying another person or group with information, materials, etc.

Handoff areas are prone to errors and confusion. People may not know when they should get involved, when to expect to receive something from other groups, and so on. Making the handoffs clear is a key benefit of using deployment flowcharts instead of some other kind of flowchart.

Handoff points are also good places to collect data to help determine how often problems occur and which type of problems occur most often. *Data Collection: Plain & Simple* can help you decide how to collect such data, and *Pareto Charts: Plain & Simple* can help you interpret it.

Deployment Flowcharts: Uses and Limitations

Uses

Deployment flowcharts help in understanding, improving, and standardizing a process that involves more than one person or group.

- Diagramming the sequence and relationship of steps using a deployment flowchart highlights the relationship between people and groups in a process
- Identifying handoffs can help improvement efforts because problems often occur where information, materials, and so on, are passed from one person or group to another
- Including decision points is important because problems also often occur at those points

Limitations

Deployment flowcharts

- Can only be used for processes with handoffs between people or groups
- Have a format in which it can be difficult to diagram steps taken when things go wrong

Exercise 6: Interpreting a Deployment Flowchart

A Medical Laboratory

In Exercise 5 you created an opportunity flowchart for a medical laboratory that wanted to find ways to reduce the time patients wait to have their blood collected. The flowchart showed three places where patients may have to wait because of cost-added-only steps

- While the test requisition form is completed
- While lab personnel get clarification of the test requisition form
- While the blood collection tray is completed

The lab personnel gathered data and discovered that the time required to have the orders explained caused the biggest problems for patients. There are three different people involved in this part of the process (lab technician, lab supervisor, and doctor), so they decided to make a deployment flowchart to learn more about the problem.

Instructions

1. Read through the steps in the flowchart on the next page.
2. Circle or highlight steps that might indicate problems in the blood collection process.

Hints

For each step, look for

- Handoffs where work could pile up
- Handoffs where what happens is unclear
- Places the lab may be able to improve the process

EXERCISE 6: INTERPRETING A DEPLOYMENT FLOWCHART

Potential Process Problems

What process problems are suggested by this flowchart? Where might delays occur? Circle the steps that indicate process problems.

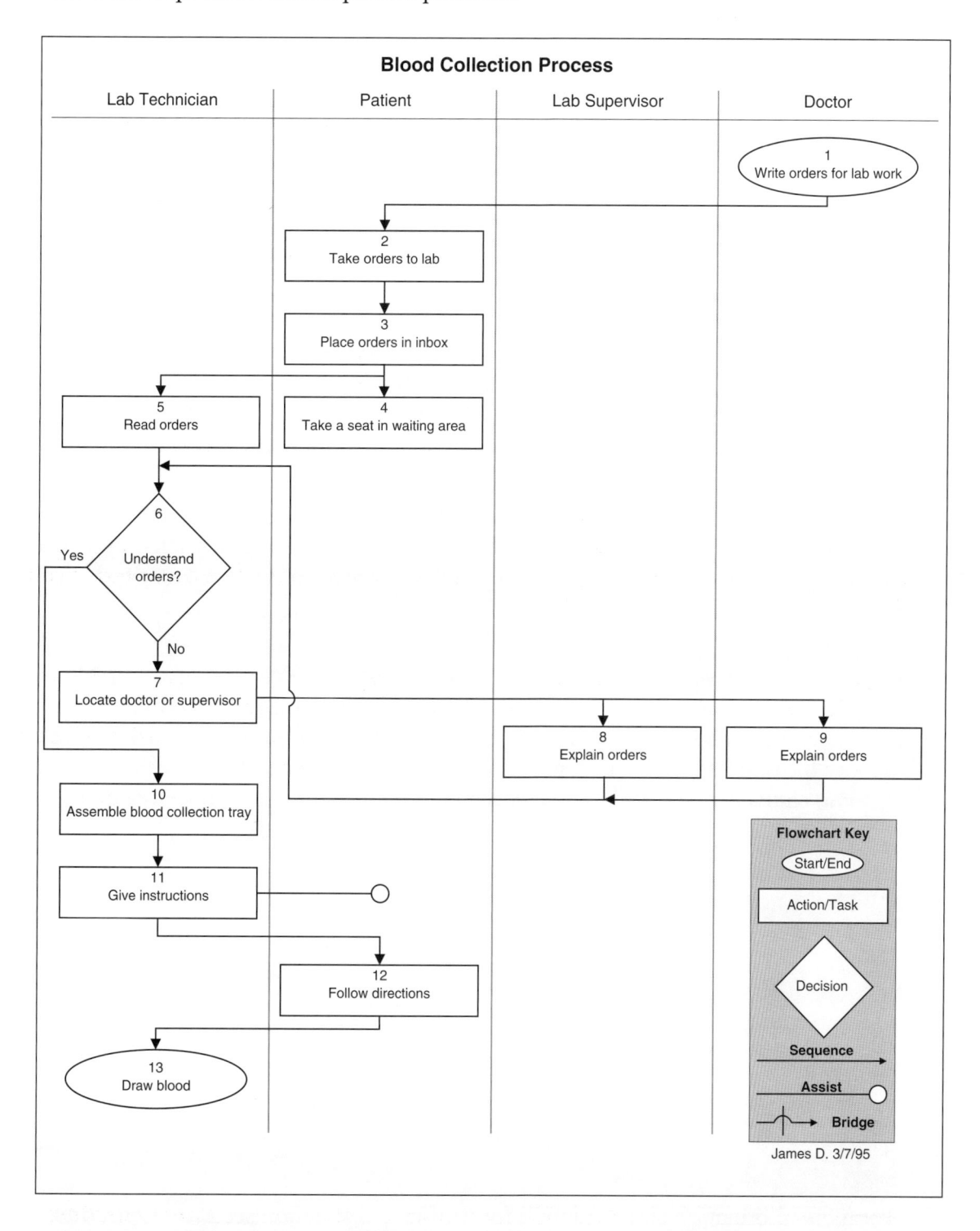

Blood Collection Process

Lab Technician	Patient	Lab Supervisor	Doctor

1. Write orders for lab work
2. Take orders to lab
3. Place orders in inbox
4. Take a seat in waiting area
5. Read orders
6. Understand orders? (Yes/No)
7. Locate doctor or supervisor
8. Explain orders
9. Explain orders
10. Assemble blood collection tray
11. Give instructions
12. Follow directions
13. Draw blood

Flowchart Key
- Start/End
- Action/Task
- Decision
- Sequence
- Assist
- Bridge

James D. 3/7/95

Flowcharts: Plain & Simple

© 2002 Oriel Incorporated. All Rights Reserved.

EXERCISE 6: INTERPRETING A DEPLOYMENT FLOWCHART

Process Problems: Answers

Comments on the Medical Laboratory Deployment Flowchart

The deployment flowchart of the blood collection process shows two places where problems could cause patients to wait.

- Between Steps 3 and 5 the orders could pile up, causing delays in the service. In processes where work moves from one person or group to another, a common problem is having work pile up at the point of the handoff.

- The handoffs between Steps 7, 8, and 9 are unclear. When lab technicians have questions about the orders, they contact either the supervisor or the doctor for more information. The flowchart does not make it clear when to contact which person.

As a result of creating this flowchart, the lab discovered that many technicians contacted both the supervisor and the doctor with their questions because it was not clear who should answer which questions. Unnecessary duplication of effort and unclear responsibilities are common problems in cross-functional processes.

The lab staff decided to collect data to understand the kinds of questions that occur in Step 6. They will use the data to establish criteria for when lab technicians can resolve problems themselves, when they can go to the supervisor, and when they need to call the doctor.

The purpose of flowcharts is to deepen understanding of the current situation. More investigation is often needed to verify the nature of the problem. Observation can verify that a potential problem actually exists, and that the flowchart really does match the way the process works. But sometimes other tools—such as checksheets, time plots, or Pareto charts*—are needed to help deepen the understanding of the problem.

*For more information on useful tools for further investigation see *Data Collection: Plain & Simple*, *Time Plots: Plain & Simple*, and *Pareto Charts: Plain & Simple*.

EXERCISE 6: INTERPRETING A DEPLOYMENT FLOWCHART

Process Problems: Answers

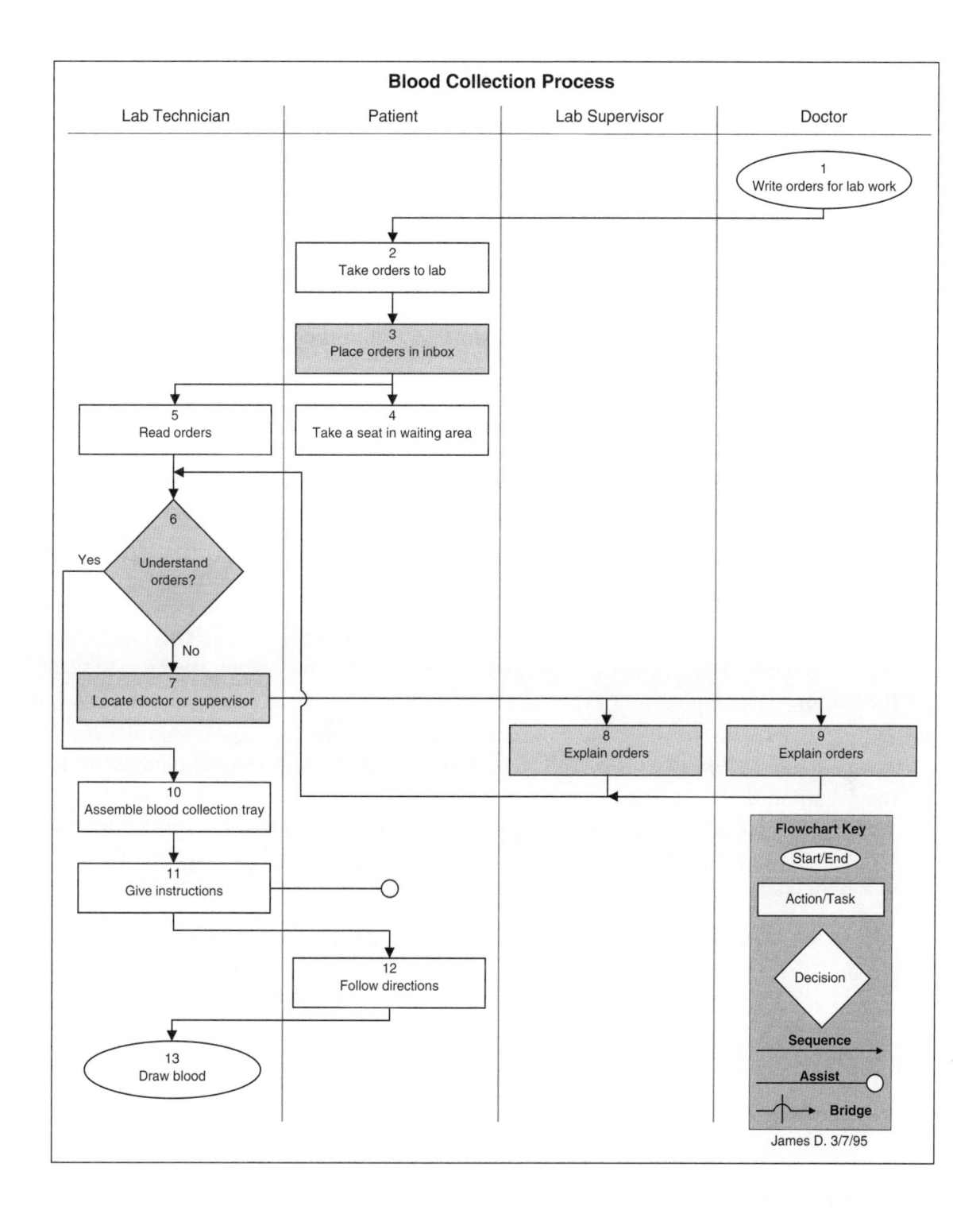

Blood Collection Process

Lab Technician	Patient	Lab Supervisor	Doctor

1. Write orders for lab work (Doctor)
2. Take orders to lab (Patient)
3. Place orders in inbox (Patient)
4. Take a seat in waiting area (Patient)
5. Read orders (Lab Technician)
6. Understand orders? (Decision — Lab Technician)
   - Yes → 10
   - No → 7
7. Locate doctor or supervisor (Lab Technician)
8. Explain orders (Lab Supervisor)
9. Explain orders (Doctor)
10. Assemble blood collection tray (Lab Technician)
11. Give instructions (Lab Technician — assists Patient)
12. Follow directions (Patient)
13. Draw blood (Lab Technician)

Flowchart Key
- Start/End
- Action/Task
- Decision
- Sequence →
- Assist ○
- Bridge

James D. 3/7/95

Flowcharts: Plain & Simple

91

© 2002 Oriel Incorporated. All Rights Reserved.

EXERCISE 6: INTERPRETING A DEPLOYMENT FLOWCHART

SUMMARY: Exercise 6

Key Points About Interpreting Deployment Flowcharts

This exercise showed a deployment flowchart for a medical laboratory's blood collection process. Exercise 5 showed both detailed and opportunity flowcharts for the same process. In each case, something different could be learned about the process and the problems that were occurring.

Each flowchart covered in Exercises 5 and 6 helped the lab identify process problems that could cause waiting time for patients.

- The opportunity flowchart showed where extra steps had been added that could cause waits
- The deployment flowchart identified unclear handoffs that might cause delays

It is important to realize that the nature of the problem or question, not the nature of the process, determines which type of flowchart to use.

The main things you should remember from this exercise are

- In order to suggest process problems, flowcharts have to capture the process as it actually works.
- It is very important for the people who carry out different steps in the process to help create the flowchart. The discussion about process steps often uncovers assumptions, misunderstandings, or unshared expectations which contribute to problems.
- Deployment flowcharts can show steps where things sit and wait. Often collecting data on the length of the wait and reasons for the wait can uncover process problems.
- Steps that exist to deal with unclear responsibilities, missing information, and other things that go wrong often add significant amounts of time to a process. Data can confirm how much time is added and can help you further focus the problem.

EXERCISE 6: INTERPRETING A DEPLOYMENT FLOWCHART

SECTION D: DEPLOYMENT FLOWCHARTS

Construction Techniques

Techniques for Constructing Deployment Flowcharts

- Use **arrows** on all **lines** to show clear direction of flow. Arrows, not step numbers, show the flow.

- Use **verbs** to label **task or activity steps**. Verbs force you to make it clear exactly what is supposed to happen.

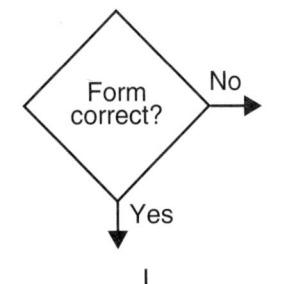

- Use **questions** to label **decision diamonds**. Questions force you to make the decisions clear.

- Include **more than one exit** on **decision diamonds**. Decisions always have two or more possible choices.

- **Label exits** from decision diamonds.

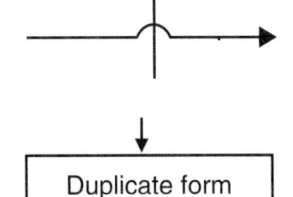

- Use a **bridge** when one **flowline** crosses another. Bridges help avoid confusion by showing where each line flows.

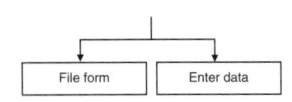

- Draw flowlines from the **bottom** of one activity step into the **top** of the next step.

- When two tasks occur at the same time, **draw the steps in parallel**.

- An **assist circle** shows people or groups that are involved in a step but don't have the lead. The circle must be connected to the box in the column of the person with lead responsibility.

- **Rounded boxes** indicate **meetings** and cover the columns for everyone involved. The flowline goes into the box in the column of the person with lead responsibility.

- A **drop shadow** on a box indicates that a **more detailed flowchart** exists for that step. Drop shadows can be used in any type of flowchart.

Flowcharts: Plain & Simple

© 2002 Oriel Incorporated. All Rights Reserved.

SECTION D: DEPLOYMENT FLOWCHARTS

Construction Example

This flowchart was created by hospital staff who wanted to make sure there was shared understanding of what happens when a doctor tells the nursing staff to give medication to a patient immediately. Notice how the different construction techniques are used in this example.

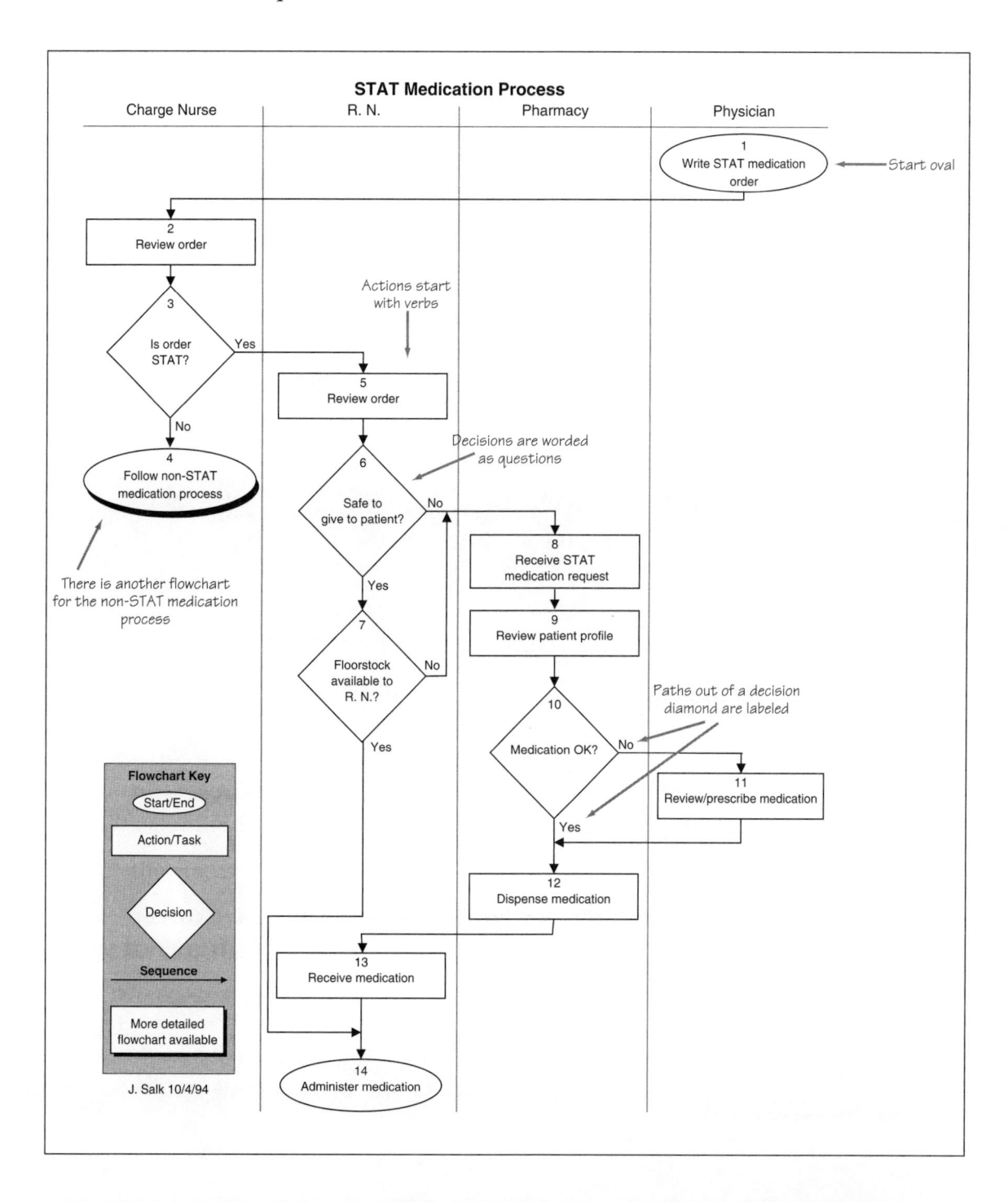

STAT Medication Process

Charge Nurse	R. N.	Pharmacy	Physician

1. Write STAT medication order ← Start oval
2. Review order
3. Is order STAT? — No → 4. Follow non-STAT medication process (There is another flowchart for the non-STAT medication process)
   — Yes → 5. Review order (Actions start with verbs)
6. Safe to give to patient? (Decisions are worded as questions) — No → 8. Receive STAT medication request → 9. Review patient profile → 10. Medication OK? — No → 11. Review/prescribe medication (Paths out of a decision diamond are labeled)
   — Yes → 7. Floorstock available to R. N.? — No → 8 (as above)
   — Yes → 13. Receive medication → 14. Administer medication
10. Medication OK? — Yes → 12. Dispense medication → 13. Receive medication

Flowchart Key
- Start/End (oval)
- Action/Task (rectangle)
- Decision (diamond)
- Sequence (arrow)
- More detailed flowchart available

J. Salk 10/4/94

Flowcharts: Plain & Simple   95

© 2002 Oriel Incorporated. All Rights Reserved.

Exercise 7: Identifying Construction Problems

Invoicing Process

The flowchart on the next page was created by a team of salespeople, accounting staff, and a major customer of the organization. The team was trying to reduce the number of accounts that were more than 30 days overdue. To understand more about payment delays, they combined a flowchart of the organization's invoicing process with steps in the customer's payment process. They wanted to use the combined flowchart to see how the steps in the two processes related to one another.

Instructions

Use the checklist below to help you judge the flowchart on page 97.

1. Look over the flowchart.
2. On the checklist below, check each technique that is consistently followed in the flowchart. If a technique does not apply, write "NA" next to the box.
3. Unchecked items are construction problems in the flowchart.
4. List additional construction problems.

Deployment Flowchart Construction Techniques

- ❐ Use single arrows on all lines to show clear direction of flow
- ❐ Use verbs in labeling task or activity boxes
- ❐ Use questions in labeling decision diamonds
- ❐ Include more than one exit on decision diamonds
- ❐ Label exits from decision diamonds
- ❐ Use a bridge when one flowline crosses another
- ❐ Place steps and draw flowlines so time flows from top to bottom of the chart
- ❐ Draw the steps in parallel when two tasks occur at the same time

EXERCISE 7: IDENTIFYING CONSTRUCTION PROBLEMS

Construction Problems Example

Identify the problems with the way the flowchart below is drawn.

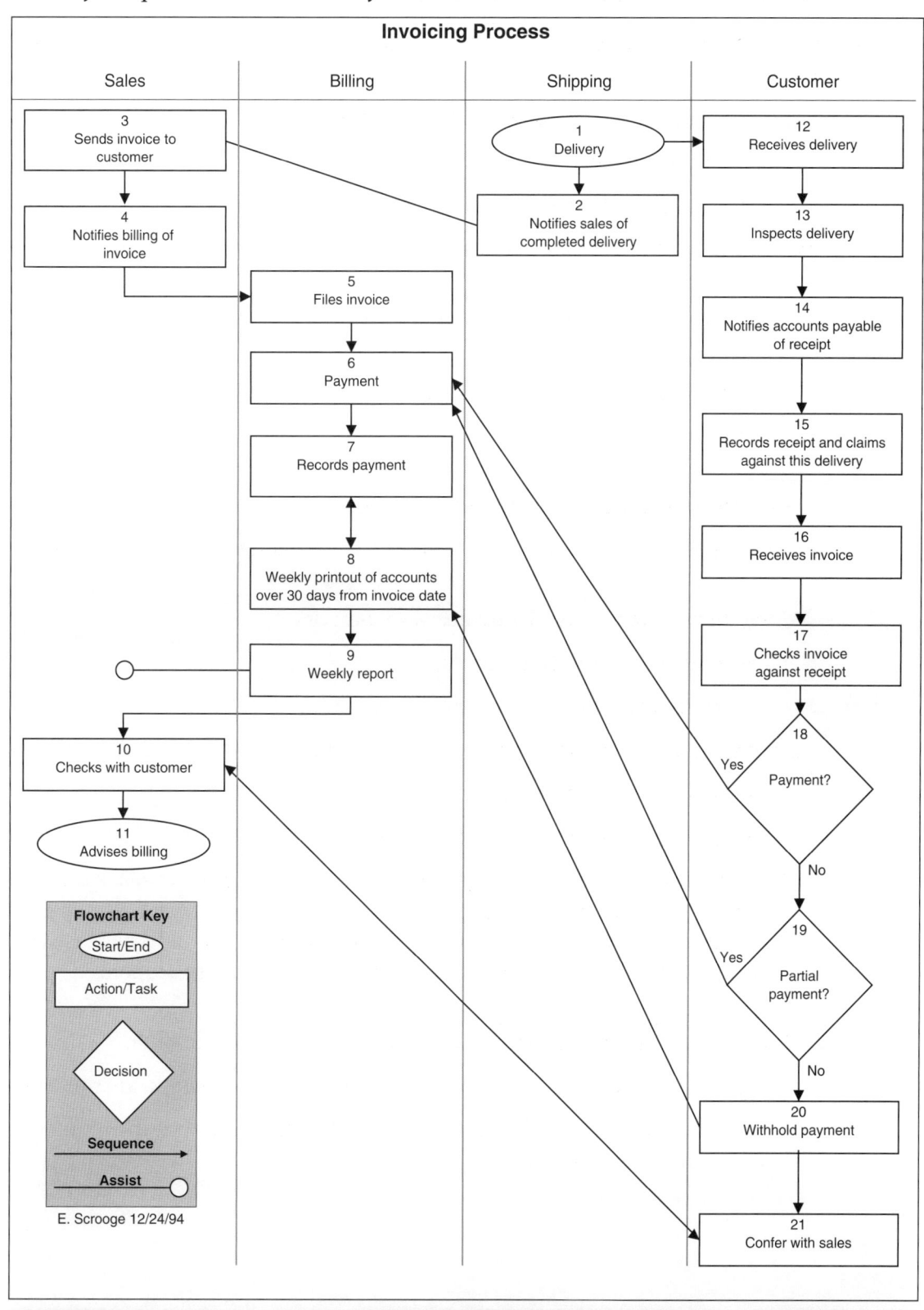

Invoicing Process

Sales	Billing	Shipping	Customer

- 1. Delivery
- 2. Notifies sales of completed delivery
- 3. Sends invoice to customer
- 4. Notifies billing of invoice
- 5. Files invoice
- 6. Payment
- 7. Records payment
- 8. Weekly printout of accounts over 30 days from invoice date
- 9. Weekly report
- 10. Checks with customer
- 11. Advises billing
- 12. Receives delivery
- 13. Inspects delivery
- 14. Notifies accounts payable of receipt
- 15. Records receipt and claims against this delivery
- 16. Receives invoice
- 17. Checks invoice against receipt
- 18. Payment?
- 19. Partial payment?
- 20. Withhold payment
- 21. Confer with sales

Flowchart Key
- Start/End
- Action/Task
- Decision
- Sequence
- Assist

E. Scrooge 12/24/94

Flowcharts: Plain & Simple 97

EXERCISE 7: IDENTIFYING CONSTRUCTION PROBLEMS

Construction Problems: Answers

Deployment Flowchart Construction Techniques

Only two of the boxes are checked. The other techniques either do not apply or are not followed consistently.

- ❏ Use single arrows on all lines to show clear direction of flow
    - The flow is not clear
    - There is no arrow between Steps 2 and 3
    - Two-headed arrows between Steps 7 and 8, and between Steps 10 and 21, are confusing
    - There are two arrows coming out of Step 1

- ❏ Use verbs to label task or activity boxes
    - Verbs are missing in Steps 1, 6, 8, and 9

- ❏ Use questions in labeling decision diamonds
    - The question in Step 18 does not make clear what decision is being made

- ☑ Include more than one exit on decision diamonds
- ☑ Label exits from decision diamonds
- **NA** ❏ Use a bridge when one flowline crosses another
- ❏ Place steps and draw flowlines so time flows from top to bottom of the chart
    - Time does not flow down the chart.
    - The steps that follow Steps 2, 18, 19, 20, and 21 are higher on the chart.
    - A common mistake in creating a deployment flowchart is to place the first step in a column at the top of that column. Instead, only the first step or steps in the process should appear at the top. All other steps should be placed further down the page depending on where they occur in sequence.

- ❏ Draw the steps in parallel when two tasks occur at the same time
    - Step 1 flows sideways to Step 12, but the tasks do not occur at the same time
    - Steps 2 and 12 occur at the same time (right after Step 1), but they are not shown in parallel on the chart

EXERCISE 7: IDENTIFYING CONSTRUCTION PROBLEMS

Construction Problems: Answers

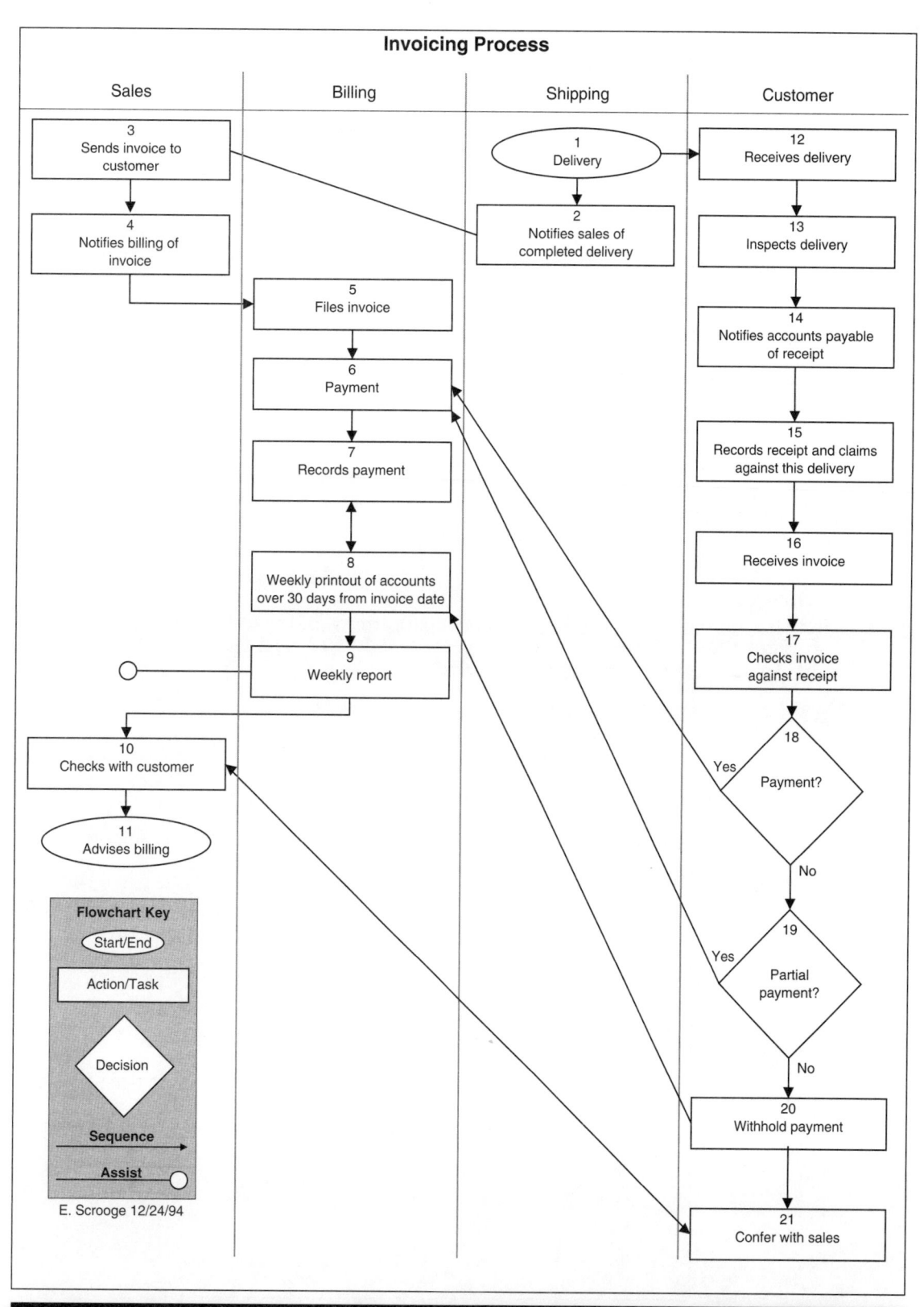

Invoicing Process

Sales	Billing	Shipping	Customer

Sales
- 3 — Sends invoice to customer
- 4 — Notifies billing of invoice
- 10 — Checks with customer
- 11 — Advises billing

Billing
- 5 — Files invoice
- 6 — Payment
- 7 — Records payment
- 8 — Weekly printout of accounts over 30 days from invoice date
- 9 — Weekly report

Shipping
- 1 — Delivery
- 2 — Notifies sales of completed delivery

Customer
- 12 — Receives delivery
- 13 — Inspects delivery
- 14 — Notifies accounts payable of receipt
- 15 — Records receipt and claims against this delivery
- 16 — Receives invoice
- 17 — Checks invoice against receipt
- 18 — Payment? (Yes → 6; No → 19)
- 19 — Partial payment? (Yes → 6; No → 20)
- 20 — Withhold payment
- 21 — Confer with sales

Flowchart Key
- Start/End (oval)
- Action/Task (rectangle)
- Decision (diamond)
- Sequence →
- Assist ─○

E. Scrooge 12/24/94

Flowcharts: Plain & Simple

99

© 2002 Oriel Incorporated. All Rights Reserved.

EXERCISE 7: IDENTIFYING CONSTRUCTION PROBLEMS

Invoicing Process Flowchart Improvements

The flowchart on the next page is one way to improve the invoicing process flowchart.

- The flow is clear
  - There is an arrow between Steps 2 and 3.
  - There are no two-headed arrows. Notice that the relationship between sales and the customer in Step 10 is now shown with an assist, not a two-headed arrow.
  - Flowlines exiting Steps 1 and 3 branch to avoid the confusion of having more than one flowline going into or out of a step.

- Steps 1, 6, 8, and 9 have verbs
- The question in Step 18, a decision diamond, now makes the decision clear
- Time flows down the chart
  - Only Step 1 is at the top of a column
  - The backward flow from Step 19 to Step 6 violates this rule, but it was left in so all the steps would fit on one page
  - Flowlines enter the top of activity boxes and exit out the bottom

- Steps that occur at the same time (Steps 2 and 12, and Steps 4 and 16) are parallel

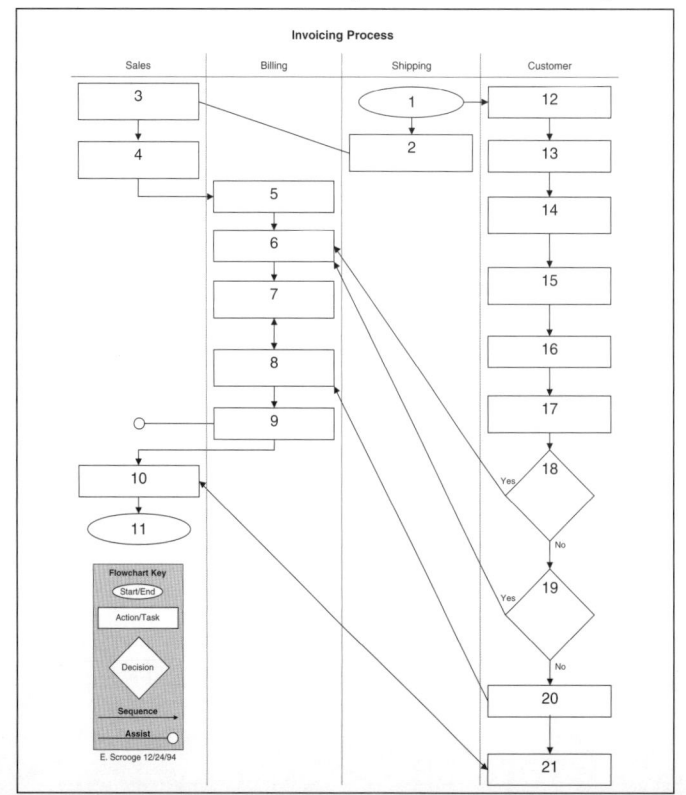

100   **Flowcharts: Plain & Simple**

© 2002 Oriel Incorporated. All Rights Reserved.

EXERCISE 7: IDENTIFYING CONSTRUCTION PROBLEMS

Construction Problems: Revised Flowchart

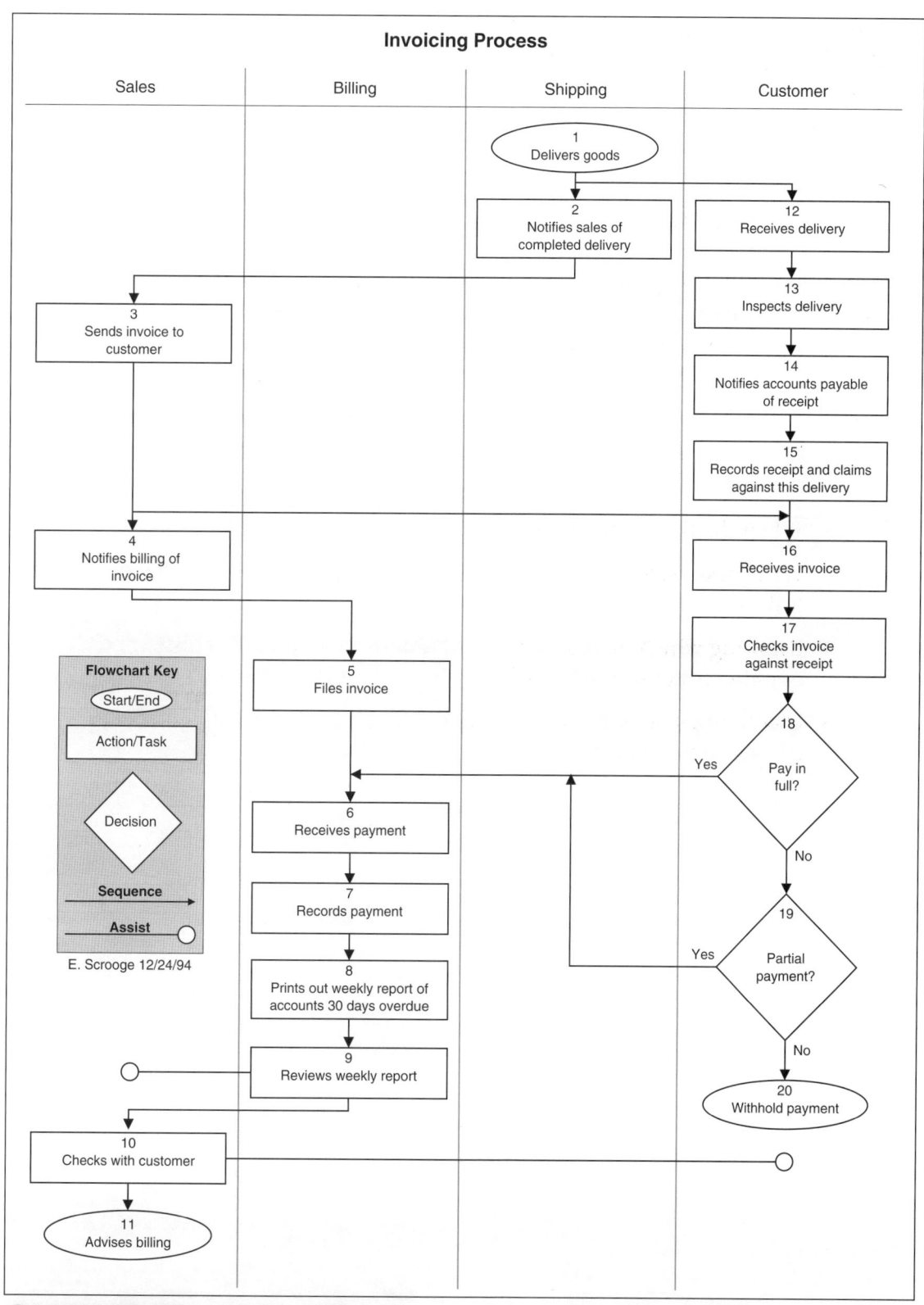

Invoicing Process

Sales	Billing	Shipping	Customer

1. Delivers goods (Shipping)
2. Notifies sales of completed delivery (Shipping)
3. Sends invoice to customer (Sales)
4. Notifies billing of invoice (Sales)
5. Files invoice (Billing)
6. Receives payment (Billing)
7. Records payment (Billing)
8. Prints out weekly report of accounts 30 days overdue (Billing)
9. Reviews weekly report (Billing)
10. Checks with customer (Sales)
11. Advises billing (Sales)
12. Receives delivery (Customer)
13. Inspects delivery (Customer)
14. Notifies accounts payable of receipt (Customer)
15. Records receipt and claims against this delivery (Customer)
16. Receives invoice (Customer)
17. Checks invoice against receipt (Customer)
18. Pay in full? (Decision)
    - Yes → to 6
19. Partial payment? (Decision)
    - Yes → to 6
    - No → 20
20. Withhold payment

Flowchart Key
- Start/End (oval)
- Action/Task (rectangle)
- Decision (diamond)
- Sequence →
- Assist ○

E. Scrooge 12/24/94

SUMMARY: Exercise 7

Flowcharts: Plain & Simple

101

© 2002 Oriel Incorporated. All Rights Reserved.

EXERCISE 7: IDENTIFYING CONSTRUCTION PROBLEMS
Key Points in Identifying Deployment Flowchart Problems

This exercise showed a deployment flowchart that was the result of combining a flowchart of an organization's invoicing process with steps in the customer's payment process. Because they wanted to reduce the number of accounts that were more than 30 days overdue, it was a good idea to look at both the company's and the customer's parts of the process.

Unfortunately, the flowchart that resulted was difficult to follow. The sequence of the steps was unclear because the steps for each group began at the top of the column. Steps were not placed in sequence. The nature of the tasks and decisions was also unclear because wording was inconsistent. Until the flowchart was redrawn, it was difficult to know how the two processes related to one another.

The main things you should remember from this exercise are

- Construction problems make it more difficult to interpret a deployment flowchart
- When the flow is not clear, it is difficult to follow the process
- When task boxes do not include verbs it is difficult to know exactly what the task is
- Knowing which path to take out of a decision diamond is difficult if the question is not worded clearly
- Combining two flowcharts into one must be done carefully to avoid construction problems

When You Can Use a Deployment Flowchart

Your Own Examples

List your own work processes where you could use a deployment flowchart. Think of processes where it is important to coordinate the efforts of different people or groups who are involved in different parts of the process.

-

-

-

-

Exercise 8: Creating a Deployment Flowchart

Car Repair Process

Use the cartoon on the next page to create a deployment flowchart of the car repair process. The construction steps are described below and are also in the deployment flowcharts section of the **Flowcharts Quick Reminder**.

Materials Needed

- One **Flowcharts: Plain & Simple Template**
- Small self-stick notes

Instructions

1. Look over the cartoon.
2. Decide on the level of detail needed.
3. Write the steps of the process on self-stick notes, one step per note.
   - Start activity steps with verbs
   - Word decisions as questions
4. Decide on the starting and ending steps.
5. Create columns on the flowchart template for the key people or functions in the process. In this process there are three people:

   Customer   Auto Shop Office Employee   Mechanic

   - List the names of these people across the top of the template
   - Draw lines from top to bottom to create three columns
6. Arrange the steps on the template.
   - Place the self-stick note for the first step in the column of the person or group responsible for it.
   - Place each succeeding step lower than the preceding step and in the column of the person or group responsible for it.
   - Check the arrangement. Make sure that time flows down the page, the steps are in the correct columns, and there are no missing steps.
7. Identify additional decision diamonds.
8. Develop alternative paths out of decision diamonds.
9. If necessary, rearrange columns to simplify the chart.
10. Add flowlines and arrows.
11. Number the steps.
12. Check construction again using the construction techniques in the **Flowcharts Quick Reminder**; make corrections as necessary.

EXERCISE 8: CREATING A DEPLOYMENT FLOWCHART

Fixing a Car

1 Hear clunking

2 _____

3 _____

4 _____

5 _____

6 _____

7 _____

8 _____

9 _____

10 _____

11 _____

12 _____

Flowcharts: Plain & Simple 105

© 2002 Oriel Incorporated. All Rights Reserved.

EXERCISE 8: CREATING A DEPLOYMENT FLOWCHART

Deployment Flowchart: Answers

Here is one way the deployment flowchart could be drawn. Your flowchart will probably be somewhat different. You may have labeled the steps differently or included decision diamonds.

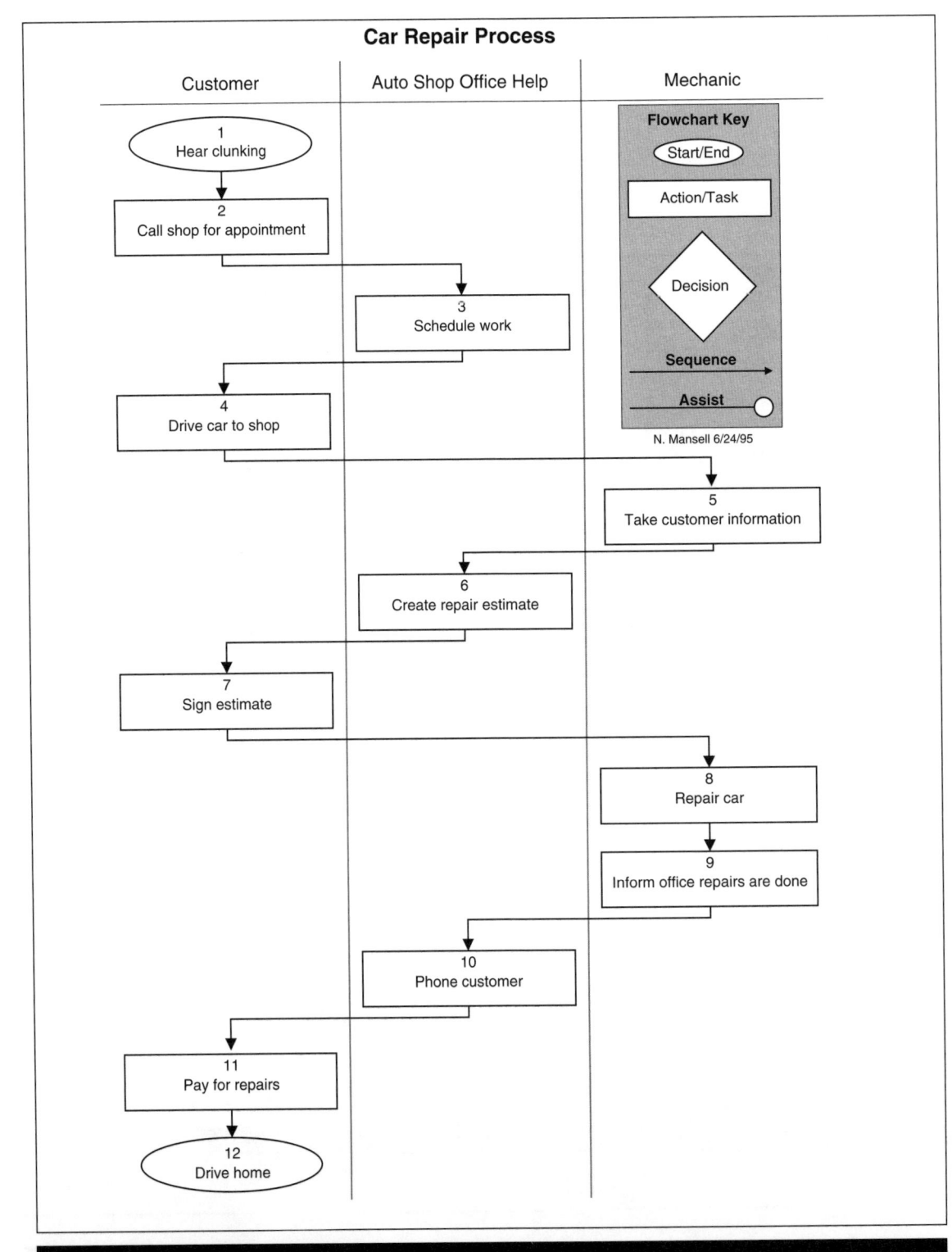

Car Repair Process

Customer	Auto Shop Office Help	Mechanic
1. Hear clunking		
2. Call shop for appointment		
	3. Schedule work	
4. Drive car to shop		
		5. Take customer information
	6. Create repair estimate	
7. Sign estimate		
		8. Repair car
		9. Inform office repairs are done
	10. Phone customer	
11. Pay for repairs		
12. Drive home		

Flowchart Key
- Start/End (oval)
- Action/Task (rectangle)
- Decision (diamond)
- Sequence (arrow)
- Assist (line with circle)

N. Mansell 6/24/95

Flowcharts: Plain & Simple

© 2002 Oriel Incorporated. All Rights Reserved.

SUMMARY: Exercise 8

Key Points About Creating a Deployment Flowchart

In this exercise you created a deployment flowchart for a car repair process. Your flowchart may have looked a little different than the one shown in the answer. For instance, you may have used the assist symbol to show that the customer was involved in Step 5, "Take customer information," even though the mechanic had the main responsibility. You may also have interpreted some of the cartoon steps differently than in the answer.

You should still have had a flowchart that showed the flow of steps in the process moving back and forth among the three people involved: the customer, office employee, and the mechanic. The process should have started when the customer heard the clunking and ended when she drove her humming car home.

The main things you should remember from this exercise are

- It can be hard to draw a flowchart for a process you don't know; the better you know a process the easier it is to make a flowchart
- Deciding how to arrange the steps is not as easy as it looks
- Steps often need to be moved around while you create the flowchart
- A deployment flowchart helps make it clear how the different people in a process relate to one another
- A deployment flowchart makes it clear who is responsible for each step in the process

Section D: Quick Check

Review of Key Questions

Here are the questions listed at the beginning of this section. Check to make sure you can answer them. If you aren't sure about any of the answers, you may want to review this section before you continue.

- What is a deployment flowchart?

- When would I use a deployment flowchart?

- What kinds of process problems will a deployment flowchart help me see?

- What are the critical components of a deployment flowchart?

- What steps are needed to create a deployment flowchart?

HIGHLIGHTS

HIGHLIGHTS

Flowchart Basics

Definition

A flowchart is a picture of the sequence of steps in a process. Different steps or actions are represented by boxes or other symbols.

Purposes of Flowcharts

- To build common understanding of a whole process
- To discover things about parts of a process not known before
- To develop process thinking
- To standardize a process by having everyone follow a single set of steps
- To improve a process

Limitations of Flowcharts

Flowcharts are useful tools for exposing problems in a process. But they cannot lead to improvement unless you work on solving those problems. Often this involves gathering data on the extent, impact, and causes of the problems.

Features of Good Flowcharts

- Process name
- Date of creation or update
- Name of person or group who created the chart
- Clear starting and ending points
- Clear direction of flow from top to bottom, left to right
- Consistent level of detail
- Numbered steps
- Key of symbol definitions

Types of Flowcharts

Detailed Flowcharts

Definition: Detailed flowcharts are one type of basic flowchart. They break the sequence of steps in a job or process into detailed substeps.

Uses: Detailed flowcharts help in understanding, improving, and standardizing a process.

Opportunity Flowcharts

Definition: An opportunity flowchart is a detailed flowchart organized to separate steps taken when things go right from steps taken when things go wrong. Steps taken when things go right move down the left side of the page; steps taken when things go wrong flow across the right side of the page.

Uses: Opportunity flowcharts help in understanding and improving a process in which things go wrong. They expose just how much work is caused by errors and missing parts or missing information.

Deployment Flowcharts

Definition: A deployment flowchart shows the detailed steps in a process and who is involved in each step. Each of the people or groups involved in a process is listed across the top of the chart and the steps are arranged in the columns of the people who carry them out.

Uses: Deployment flowcharts help in understanding, improving, and standardizing a process that involves more than one person or group.

HIGHLIGHTS

Flowchart Construction Techniques

Symbol	Meaning	Symbol	Meaning
⟶	Use arrows on all lines to show clear direction of flow	[File form] [Enter data]	When two tasks occur at the same time, draw the steps in parallel
[Complete form]	Use verbs to label task or action boxes	○──	An assist circle in a deployment flowchart shows people or groups that are involved in a step, but don't have the lead
◇ Form correct? No/Yes	Use questions to label decision diamonds. Include more than one exit on decision diamonds. Label exits from decision diamonds	(Meet to review schedule)	Rounded boxes indicate meetings in a deployment flowchart
─┴─⟶	Use a bridge when one flowline crosses another	[Follow established procedures] (with drop shadow)	A drop shadow on a box indicates that a more detailed flowchart exists for that step
[Duplicate form]	Draw flowlines from the bottom of one action step into the top of the next step	(Start)	Ovals indicate the beginning and ending steps

Flowcharts: Plain & Simple

© 2002 Oriel Incorporated. All Rights Reserved.

Glossary

Average: The sum of all of the values in a set of data divided by the number of values in the set. For example, if the values are 3, 5, 7, and 9, then 3 + 5 + 7 + 9 = 24, and 24 ÷ 4 = 6, the average for that set of data. (*See* Mean.)

Basic flowchart: A flowchart that shows the sequence of steps in a job or process. It can have different levels of detail.

Bimodal: A pattern seen on a frequency plot where the shape of the distribution has two humps instead of the more typical one hump. This frequently occurs when what we think of as one process is really a mixture of two processes.

Brainstorming: A technique used to generate a list of creative ideas. Everyone is encouraged to give any idea that comes to them. In brainstorming, ideas are not analyzed or judged.

Categorical data: Data that are labels rather than numbers. The label may describe a classification, category, or group of the item of interest. For example, for data on reasons people were absent from work, the classifications might include categories such as illness, vacation, holiday, or funeral leave. (*See also* Continuous data.)

Categorize: To group, or classify, according to a specific characteristic, e.g., color, shape, type of defect.

Cause-and-effect diagram: A tool that is used for identifying and organizing possible causes of a problem in a structured format. It is sometimes called a "fishbone" diagram because it looks like the skeleton of a fish.

Centerline: The middle line on a control chart or time plot. It represents either the average or median value of the data.

Checksheets: Forms used to collect data by making tally marks to indicate the number of times something occurs. Checksheets help standardize the data that is collected and the data collection process.

Checklists: A list of action items, steps, or elements needed for a task. The items are checked off as they are completed.

Common cause: A cause of variation that is inherent to the process.

Concentration diagram: A specific type of checksheet in which you write directly on a picture of the object about which you are collecting data.

Continuous data: Measurements that can take on any numerical value, not just whole numbers (1, 2, 3). Some measurements that could be collected as continuous data are height, weight, or temperature. (*See also* Categorical data.)

Control chart: A time plot that has a centerline and statistical control limits added. There is an upper control limit and a lower control limit. These limits allow you to quickly detect specific types of changes in a process.

Terms in this glossary come from all the learning and application guides in this series. Not all of them appear in this guide.

GLOSSARY

Control limit: A line on a control chart that indicates either the upper or lower range of the common cause variation within a process. Also called "statistical control limit."

Cost-added-only step: A step in a process that is not essential for producing the product or service. It is carried out because defects, errors, or omissions do occur or because we worry that defects, errors, or omissions might occur.

Cumulative line: A line that can be added to a Pareto chart. It shows how much, or what percentage, of the problem comes from the largest categories.

Data: Clearly defined measurements of characteristics. They are most useful when collected for the purpose of monitoring or improving a process.

Data point: A single measurement, count, or observation.

Deployment flowchart: A flowchart that shows the detailed steps in a process and which people are involved in each step.

Detailed flowchart: A flowchart that breaks the sequence of steps in a job or a process into detailed substeps.

Dot plot: A type of frequency plot that uses dots to show how often values occur in each interval. It shows the shape or distribution of the variation in the data.

80/20 Rule: In many situations, roughly 80% of the problems are caused by only 20% of the contributors. (*See also* Pareto Principle.)

5 Step Process for Data Collection: A process that ensures the collection of meaningful data and includes clarification of data collection goals, development of operational definitions, planning for data consistency and stability, beginning data collection, and continuous improvement of measurement systems.

Flowchart: A picture of the sequence of steps in a process. Different steps or actions are represented by boxes or other symbols. Common types of flowcharts include basic, opportunity, and deployment.

Frequency plot: A graphical tool that shows the shape, or distribution, of the data by showing how often different values occur. This picture makes it easier to see what is happening with the data and to identify some types of process problems.

Go-Look-See: To go to the workplace to observe the process under study.

Graph: A picture of data.

Histogram: A type of frequency plot that uses bars to show how often values occur in each interval. It shows the shape or distribution of the variation in the data.

Horizontal axis: The labeled straight line at the bottom of a graph that runs from left to right, or horizontally. It is also called the X-axis.

Terms in this glossary come from all the learning and application guides in this series. Not all of them appear in this guide.

GLOSSARY

Improvement tools: Data collection and analysis tools used to better understand and more quickly solve problems.

Individuals chart: A type of control chart used for data that is collected one value at a time, such as daily production volume or time to process each report.

Lower control limit (LCL): A value, represented by a line on a control chart, that specifies the lower limit of the results of common cause variation. Data points that fall below this value provide signals of special causes. (*See also* Upper control limit.)

Mean: (*See* Average.)

Median: The numerical midpoint of a list of numbers. It is found by rank ordering the values and locating the number that in rank is halfway between the beginning and end. If there is an odd number of values, the median is the middle value; if there is an even number of values, the median is the average of the middle two values.

Normalizing data: Turning a count into a rate or percentage so that it can more easily be compared with other values. This is used when the areas of opportunity are of unequal size. For example, since some months have more working days than others, it may make more sense to normalize the data by dividing the amount produced in a month by the number of working days in that month.

Operational definition: A precise description that tells how to get a value for the characteristic you are trying to measure.

Opportunity flowchart: A detailed flowchart organized to separate steps taken when things go right from steps taken when things go wrong.

Pareto chart: A graphical tool that helps break a big problem down into its parts and then identifies which parts are the most important.

Pareto Principle: A principle that states that, in many situations, a small number of causes account for most of the problems, while most of the causes account for only a few of the problems. (*See also* 80/20 Rule.)

Process: A series of linked steps necessary to accomplish work. A process turns inputs, such as information or raw materials, into outputs, like products, services, and reports.

R̃: R-tilde, or median R, is the median or middle value in a set of ranges.

Range: The difference between two data values. For a set of data, the range is the difference between the highest numerical value and the lowest numerical value.

Rework: Redoing some process steps or adding new steps due to defects, errors, omissions, or other quality problems.

Root cause: The deep, underlying cause of a problem in a process or system.

Terms in this glossary come from all the learning and application guides in this series. Not all of them appear in this guide.

Flowcharts: Plain & Simple

GLOSSARY

Scatter plot: A graphical tool that shows the relationship between two variables. It is sometimes referred to as a scatter diagram.

7 Step Method: A scientific approach to problem solving that involves collecting data and testing theories. It is designed to help analyze the root cause of problems in a systematic way.

Special cause: A specific or assignable cause of variation that is outside of the normal variation in a process. It is signaled by a data point falling outside of the upper control limit (UCL) or lower control limit (LCL), or by one of several defined patterns on a control chart or time plot.

Statistical control limits: (*See* Control limit.)

Stem-and-leaf plot: A type of frequency plot that captures the exact values of specific data points. Numerical values, rather than dots or x's, are used to mark each data point.

Stratification: Dividing a whole group of data into subgroups (strata) to see whether the data is different for different subgroups. This helps focus efforts on those factors that have the most impact on the problem.

Tick mark labels: The numbers that identify major units of possible data values along an axis (such as units of 1, 5, 10, 50, 100, 1000, etc.). Oftentimes, only every other (or every fourth) tick mark is labeled to keep the chart from being too cluttered.

Time plot: A graph of data in time order. It helps identify any changes that occur over time.

Time-ordered data: Characteristics that are measured, counted, or observed and recorded in the chronological order in which they occur.

Top-down flowchart: A flowchart that shows both the major steps in a process and the next level of substeps.

Upper control limit (UCL): A value, represented by a line on a control chart, that specifies the upper limit of the results of common cause variation. Data points that fall above this value provide signals of special causes. (*See also* Lower control limit.)

Value-added step: A step in a process that is essential for producing the product or service at the current level of technology.

Variable: The characteristic(s) that you are measuring.

Variation: Differences among measured values in a process.

Vertical axis: The labeled straight line at the side of a graph that runs up and down, or vertically. It is also called the Y-axis.

Work-flow diagram: A tool for collecting data on how work flows through an operation. The path of the work is recorded on a schematic of the workplace.

$\overline{X}$: X-bar is the symbol that represents the average, or mean, of a set of data.

Terms in this glossary come from all the learning and application guides in this series.
Not all of them appear in this guide.

References

Asaka, Tetsuichi and Kazuo Ozeki (eds.). *Handbook of Quality Tools: The Japanese Approach.* Cambridge, MA: Productivity Press, 1990. Short chapters on each tool, using mostly manufacturing examples. Also includes information on how to manage for quality.

Brassard, Michael. *The Memory Jogger.*™ Methuen, MA: GOAL/QPC, 1989. This pocket-sized guide gives brief descriptions, construction tips, and examples for each of the tools. A handy reminder with good practical advice and directions.

Fuller, Timothy F. "Eliminating Complexity from Work: Improving Productivity by Enhancing Quality," *National Productivity Review*, Autumn, 1985, pp. 327-344. Based on the experience of Hewlett-Packard, the author provides a model that all organizations can use to identify, measure, and eliminate complexity, thereby improving quality and productivity.

Kelly, Michael R. *Everyone's Problem Solving Handbook.* White Plains, NY: Quality Resources, 1992. This book focuses on the QI Story problem-solving method and explains the tools in this context. Most examples are non-manufacturing based.

Manufacturing Process Improvement Pocket Advisor. Knoxville, TN: QualPro, 1992. A pocket-sized reminder of how to use each tool in an improvement context. Separate editions are available for manufacturing, service, and healthcare.

Plsek, Paul E. and Arturo Onnias. *Quality Improvement Tools.* Wilton, CT: Juran Institute, Inc., 1989. An advanced set of instructional materials designed to teach the tools. The material provides a good deal of background reading on each tool and focuses on the tool's use in an improvement context.

Total Quality Transformation. Dayton, OH: QIP, Inc. and PQ Systems, Inc., 1991. A glossary-style reference book on the tools. For each tool, there is a description of the tool, an illustration, directions for when to use it, information on how to construct it, and usage tips.

Oriel Materials

All products are available from Oriel Incorporated, P.O. Box 5445, Madison, WI 53705. Phone: 1-800-669-8326.

Fundamentals of Fourth Generation Management. An eight-module, video-based instructional program that explores the basic principles of a customer focus, a scientific approach, and working together as "all one team." The program mixes video instruction with real-time exercises that emphasize key points and skills. (1993)

Joiner, Brian L. *Fourth Generation Management: The New Business Consciousness.* A book that describes how a new synthesis of management principles is being used to create rapid, sustained improvement. (New York: McGraw-Hill, 1993)

The Practical Guide to Quality. A collection of selected readings. (1993)

Running Effective Meetings. A four-hour instructional program designed to help any kind of group learn and practice basic meeting skills. (1992)

Scholtes, Peter R. et al. *The Team Handbook: How to Use Teams to Improve Quality.* A book that presents many useful details that help teams work together to make improvements. Available in English, French, Portuguese, and Spanish, and audiotape editions. A special edition for educators is also available. (1988)

The 7 Step Method Notebook. A workbook reviews the Joiner 7 Step Method for problem solving. (1990)

The Team Companion™. A set of instructional resources based on *The Team Handbook.* The materials include overheads, worksheets, Pocket Cards, Quick Reference Guides, and posters. (1991)

FLOWCHARTS
Plain & Simple

Template

Oriel®

Flowchart Template

Process under study: _____ Date: _____

Team or individual name: _____ Contact/Phone number: _____

Flowchart Key

- Start/End (oval)
- Action/Task (rectangle)
- Decision (diamond)
- Sequence (arrow)
- Bridge
- Assist
- Meeting

Flowcharts: Plain & Simple

Template

© 1995 Joiner Associates Inc. All Rights Reserved.

When to Use Which Flowchart

When you want	Use
A quick outline of the big steps in a process	Basic flowchart with major steps
A deep look at a process which involves mostly one person or group	Basic flowchart with detailed steps
To understand or improve a process that has a lot of rework, inspections, approvals, missing parts, or missing information	Opportunity flowchart
To understand or improve a process involving several people or groups	Deployment flowchart

FLOWCHARTS
Plain & Simple

Template

oriel®

Flowchart Template

Process under study: _____ Date: _____

Team or individual name: _____ Contact/Phone number: _____

Flowchart Key

- Start/End
- Action/Task
- Decision
- Sequence
- Bridge
- Assist
- Meeting

Flowcharts: Plain & Simple — Template

© 1995 Joiner Associates Inc. All Rights Reserved.

When to Use Which Flowchart

When you want	Use
A quick outline of the big steps in a process	Basic flowchart with major steps
A deep look at a process which involves mostly one person or group	Basic flowchart with detailed steps
To understand or improve a process that has a lot of rework, inspections, approvals, missing parts, or missing information	Opportunity flowchart
To understand or improve a process involving several people or groups	Deployment flowchart

FLOWCHARTS
Plain & Simple

Template

oriel®

Flowchart Template

Process under study: _____ Date: _____

Team or individual name: _____ Contact/Phone number: _____

Flowchart Key

- Start/End (oval)
- Action/Task (rectangle)
- Decision (diamond)
- Sequence (arrow)
- Bridge
- Assist
- Meeting

Template

Flowcharts: Plain & Simple

© 1995 Joiner Associates Inc. All Rights Reserved.

When to Use Which Flowchart

When you want	Use
A quick outline of the big steps in a process	Basic flowchart with major steps
A deep look at a process which involves mostly one person or group	Basic flowchart with detailed steps
To understand or improve a process that has a lot of rework, inspections, approvals, missing parts, or missing information	Opportunity flowchart
To understand or improve a process involving several people or groups	Deployment flowchart

1-800-669-8326   1-608-238-8134

FLOWCHARTS

Plain & Simple

Template

oriel®

Flowchart Template

Process under study: _____ Date: _____

Team or individual name: _____ Contact/Phone number: _____

Flowchart Key

- Start/End (oval)
- Action/Task (rectangle)
- Decision (diamond)
- Sequence (arrow)
- Bridge
- Assist
- Meeting

Flowcharts: Plain & Simple

Template

© 1995 Joiner Associates Inc. All Rights Reserved.

When to Use Which Flowchart

When you want	Use
A quick outline of the big steps in a process	Basic flowchart with major steps
A deep look at a process which involves mostly one person or group	Basic flowchart with detailed steps
To understand or improve a process that has a lot of rework, inspections, approvals, missing parts, or missing information	Opportunity flowchart
To understand or improve a process involving several people or groups	Deployment flowchart

1-800-669-8326   1-608-238-8134

Reorder No. 08021

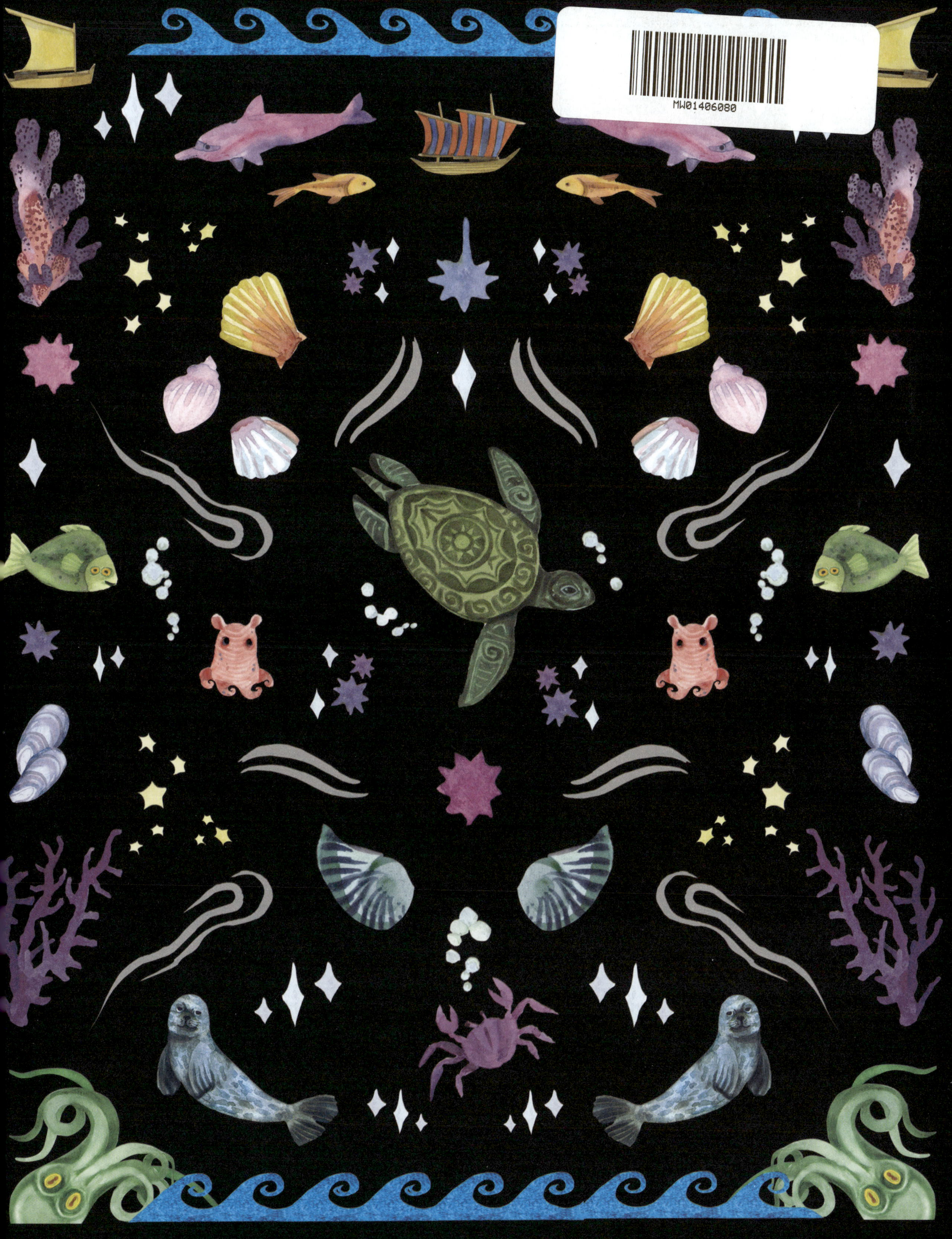

To Bryn, Soren, and Romilly.–C. C-S.

To my son Sasha.–S. R.

Lore of the Deep copyright © Quarto Publishing plc 2024
Illustrations copyright © Stacey Rozich 2024
Text copyright © Claire Cock-Starkey 2024

First published in 2024 by Wide Eyed Editions, an imprint of The Quarto Group.
100 Cummings Center, Suite 265D, Beverly, MA 01915, USA.
T +1 978-282-9590 www.Quarto.com

The right of Claire Cock-Starkey and Stacey Rozich to be identified as the author and illustrator of this work, respectively, has been asserted by them both in accordance with the Copyright, Designs and Patents Act, 1988 (United Kingdom).
All rights reserved.

No part of this publication may be reproduced, stored in a retrieval system, or transmitted, in any form, or by any means, electrical, mechanical, photocopying, recording, or otherwise without the prior written permission of the publisher or a license permitting restricted copying.

ISBN 978-0-7112-8771-6
eISBN 978-0-7112-8773-0

Illustrated with watercolor
Set in Budidaya and Slopes

Designed by Vanessa Lovegrove and Lyli Feng
Edited by Corinne Lucas
Commissioned by Alex Hithersay
Production by Dawn Cameron
Art Director: Karissa Santos
Published by Debbie Foy

Manufactured in Guangdong, China TT072024
1 3 5 7 9 8 6 4 2

LORE OF THE DEEP

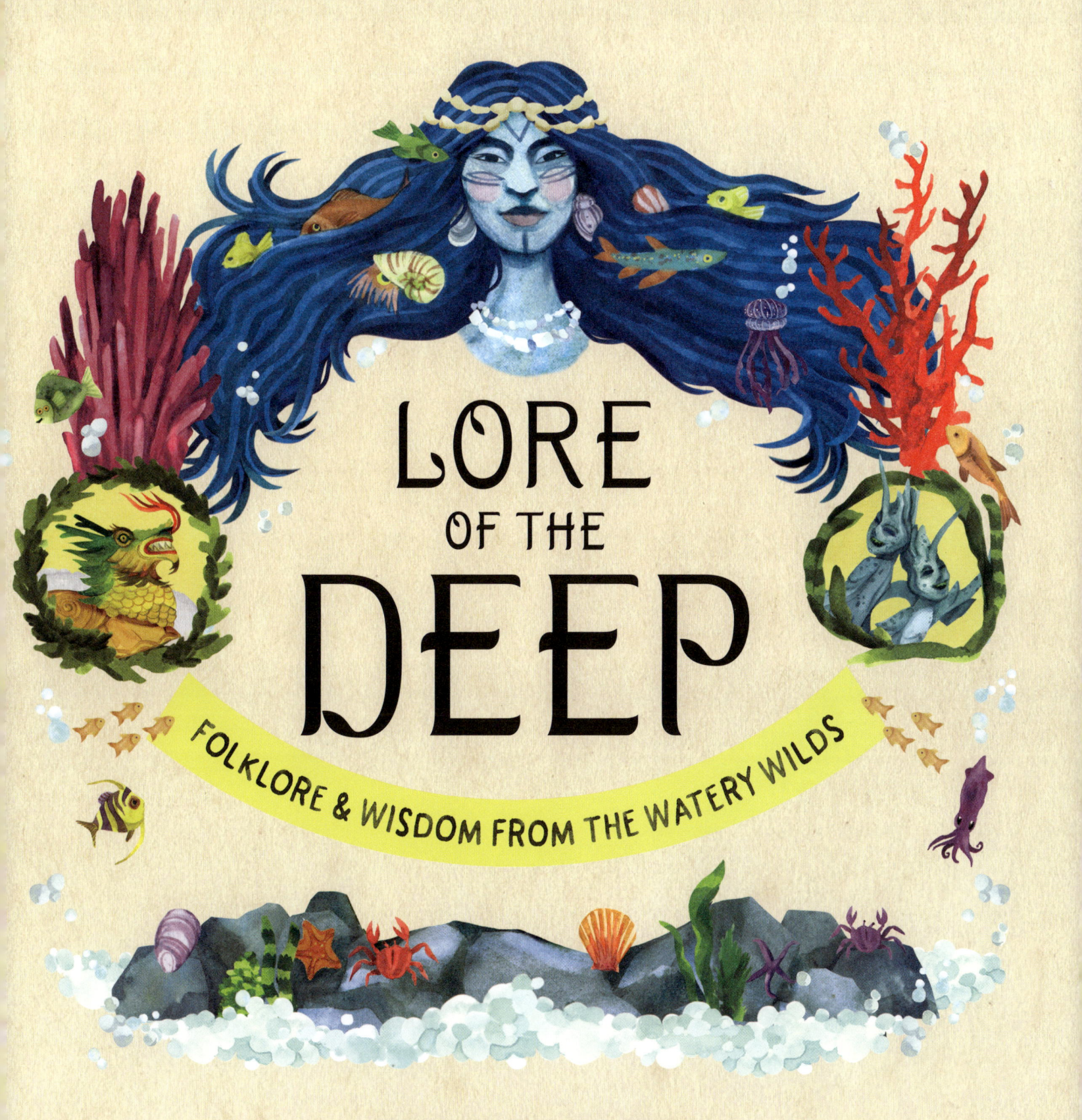

FOLKLORE & WISDOM FROM THE WATERY WILDS

CLAIRE COCK-STARKEY
ILLUSTRATED BY STACEY ROZICH

WIDE EYED EDITIONS

CONTENTS

MYTHICAL SEAS AND OCEANS
THE POEM FROM THE SEA, a Japanese tale	8
NAMING THE SEAS	10
PRIMORDIAL OCEANS	12
SEA GODS AND GODDESSES	14
SPIRITS OF THE SEA	16
SHAPE-SHIFTERS OF THE OCEANS	18

CREATURES OF THE SEAS AND OCEANS
ARION AND THE DOLPHIN, a tale from ancient Greece	20
WHALES, DOLPHINS, SHARKS, AND RAYS	22
FISH AND SEA CREATURES	24
SEALS AND TURTLES	26
SEABIRDS	28
EERIE CREATURES OF THE DEEP	30

SEAFARERS
SINBAD THE SAILOR AND THE ROC, an Arabian folktale	32
SAILOR LORE	34
PIRATE LORE	36
FISHING LORE	38
LEGENDARY VOYAGES	40
BOAT LORE	42

STORMY WATERS

A WHISPER IN THE WIND, an American tale	44
WAVES AND WHIRLPOOLS	46
STORMS AND TYPHOONS	48
SEA WINDS AND MISTS	50
SEA-WEATHER LORE	52

OCEAN LANDSCAPES

WHY THE SEA IS SALTY, an Ilocano Filipino tale	54
BEACHES AND DUNES	56
SEA CAVES AND COVES	58
COASTAL CLIFFS	60
SUBMERGED CITIES, ISLANDS, AND CONTINENTS	62
MYTHICAL ISLANDS	64

OMINOUS OCEANS

ASSIPATTLE AND THE STOOR WORM, a tale from the Orkney Islands	66
GHOST SHIPS	68
MARITIME MISCHIEF-MAKERS	70
SEA MONSTERS AND SEA SERPENTS	72
PERILOUS STRETCHES OF WATER	74

GLOSSARY	76
INDEX	77

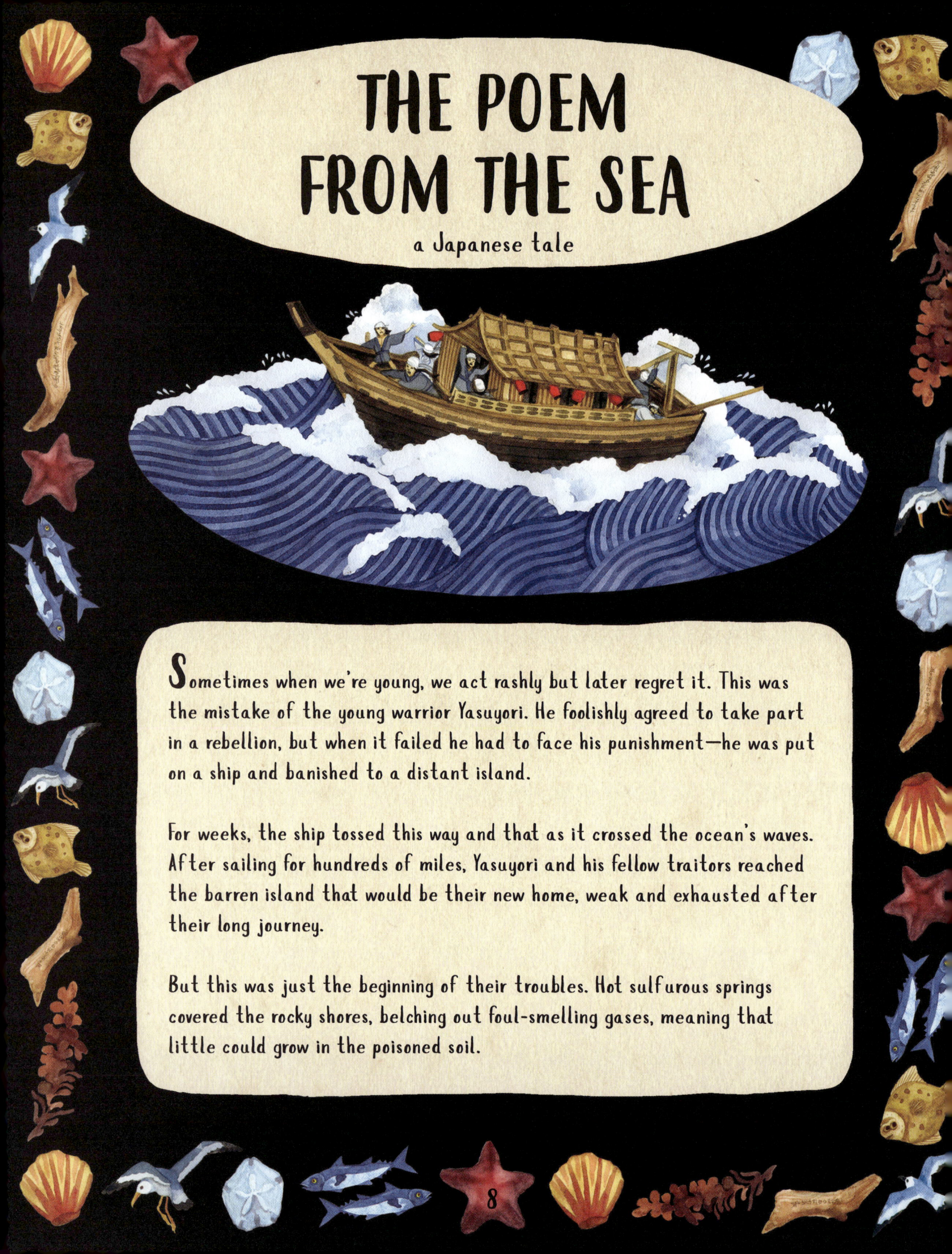

THE POEM FROM THE SEA

a Japanese tale

Sometimes when we're young, we act rashly but later regret it. This was the mistake of the young warrior Yasuyori. He foolishly agreed to take part in a rebellion, but when it failed he had to face his punishment—he was put on a ship and banished to a distant island.

For weeks, the ship tossed this way and that as it crossed the ocean's waves. After sailing for hundreds of miles, Yasuyori and his fellow traitors reached the barren island that would be their new home, weak and exhausted after their long journey.

But this was just the beginning of their troubles. Hot sulfurous springs covered the rocky shores, belching out foul-smelling gases, meaning that little could grow in the poisoned soil.

As the hot sun beat down each day on to the shadeless beach, Yasuyori and his companions desperately searched for food. They picked dried seaweed off the rocks and scoured rockpools for measly fish and skinny crabs, anything to lessen their gnawing hunger.

It was a miserable life with no end in sight. Yasuyori sat down, looking out over the endless expanse of ocean, and thought of his mother. He knew that she didn't know where he'd been taken and his heart ached when he thought of her unhappiness.

In his despair, he picked up a piece of driftwood and carved a poem for his mother, expressing his love for her. He threw the message into the ocean, willing it to find its way, somehow, into her hands.

Over the next few days, Yasuyori wrote ninety-nine more heartfelt poems for his mother and entrusted them to the wild waters. The ocean took these precious notes into its currents and moved them silently and safely through its depths until, many hundreds of miles later, they reached a distant shore.

Luck was surely on Yasuyori's side, for the poems washed up at the feet of a kindly priest, who plucked one from the water. Tears sprang to his eyes as he read the beautiful words, full of love, longing, and regret.

The priest ran to find Yasuyori's mother, who fortunately lived in the same village as him, and presented her with the driftwood poems. As she read the words, she cried with joy.

The story of Yasuyori's beautiful poems soon reached the ears of Japan's emperor. He immediately sent a boat to bring the young man home from exile so Yasuyori could at last be reunited with his mother.

Thankful to be home, Yasuyori treasured his freedom and was always grateful for the kindness of the sea.

NAMING THE SEAS

The seas and oceans are known by many different names in many different languages, but typically they are named after the land, peoples, or region they border. However, there are some seas and oceans out there that have taken their names from myths, legends, or sailor lore.

The phrase "sailing the seven seas" was first used by sailors to show they'd traveled across the globe. Which seven has changed over time, depending on where the sailor was from and which era they lived in.

The Sargasso Sea in the North Atlantic was named by early explorers because the water there is covered in brown sargassum seaweed. Sailors believed it was a dangerous place because they thought the seaweed could entangle their ships and trap them forever.

NORTH PACIFIC

NORTH ATLANTIC

SOUTH PACIFIC

SOUTHERN OCEAN

For medieval Europeans, the seven seas tended to include: the Mediterranean Sea, Adriatic Sea, Black Sea, Red Sea, Arabian Sea, Caspian Sea, and the Persian Gulf. Today, the "seven seas" are considered to be all the major bodies of water on Earth: the Arctic, North Atlantic, South Atlantic, Indian, North Pacific, South Pacific, and Southern oceans.

10

In an ancient Greek myth, Zeus fell in love with Io and changed her into a white cow to protect her from his wife Hera's jealousy. But Hera found out and sent a fly to torment Io. To escape, Io swam across the Ionian Sea, which has since been named in her honor.

It's thought that the Black Sea got its name because the terrible winter storms that happen there turn the water so dark it looks black.

Ferdinand Magellan was a Portuguese explorer who organized the first expedition to sail around the world in 1519. After a difficult journey, passing through many rough seas, he finally reached an unfamiliar ocean that was still and calm. He named it the Pacific, meaning peaceful.

INDIAN OCEAN

SOUTH ATLANTIC

PRIMORDIAL OCEANS

Primordial oceans are the endless seas that were thought to exist before the land was created. They represent chaos, and many legends tell of how the universe was formed out of these swirling waters, marking the start of order in the world.

Luonnotar was a Finnish goddess who grew bored and dived into the primordial ocean. While she floated aimlessly, a duck built a nest on her knee. When Luonnotar moved the eggs fell, creating the Earth, Sun, Moon, sky, and stars.

In ancient Mesopotamia (modern-day Iraq), Tiamat was a goddess who existed in the form of an enormous, salty, primordial ocean. Her opposite was Apsu, the freshwater sea. When the waters of Tiamat and Apsu mingled, they created many new gods.

Nun is one of the oldest ancient Egyptian gods. But he also represents a tempestuous and stormy primordial ocean. His child—the sun god Re—emerged from the chaotic waters when the world was created.

Hindu mythology tells that the Devas (gods) had to work with their demon enemies, the Asuras, to churn the Ocean of Milk. They used a massive serpent king named Vasuki as a rope to mix the primordial oceans, and this released many wonderful gifts, including an elixir of immortality.

In Oceania's Papua New Guinea, the Iatmul people say that the world was formed after an ancestral crocodile dove into the primordial ocean. Mud from the ocean floor was carried to the surface on the crocodile's back and hardened into the land we live on today.

SEA GODS AND GODDESSES

Given the stormy nature of the ocean, it might not come as a surprise that many sea gods and goddesses are wild and unpredictable. In an effort to calm them, sailors often worship sea deities by making offerings in return for calm waters and a safe passage.

Finnish god of the seas Ahti is a gloomy character who is jealous of all the attention the sky gods get. Sulking, he lives inside a black cliff protected by mist, creating whirlpools that cause shipwrecks. But sometimes, when he feels like being kind to humans, he gifts us fish.

For the Yoruba people of West Africa, Olokun is the "owner of the sea." Depending on the region, Olokun is either described as male, female, or as having no gender at all. They live at the bottom of the sea and symbolize the riches that come from the ocean.

For Brazilian followers of the Candomblé religion, Iemanjá is a powerful sea goddess who looks after sailors and fisherfolk. Once a year, a festival is held in her honour. People gather at the sea shore, dressed in white, and throw flowers for her into the waves.

In Chinese tradition, Mazu is goddess of the ocean. She was originally a mortal who had a vision of her father and brothers' fishing boat sinking. Taking the form of a spirit, Mazu rescued them and was turned into a goddess to forever act as a guardian to sailors and fisherfolk.

Susanoo is the god of the sea in the Japanese religion Shintoism. He was thrown out of heaven after his fierce temper caused lots of storms at sea. Now he stands guard at the entrance to the Land of the Dead, a role better suited to his wild nature.

The sheer power of the sea is represented by the Greek god of the ocean, Poseidon. Riding in a sea chariot pulled by fish-tailed horses, he wields a trident and lives in a palace in the deepest part of the ocean.

SPIRITS OF THE SEA

In many cultures across the world, people have imagined sea spirits dwelling in the oceans, but they are all different. Some are kind and helpful to sailors, while others are said to be mischievous, causing storms and keeping fish out of fisherfolk's nets.

Bucca are Cornish sea spirits or fairies that look like mermen. To get in their good favor, fisherfolk either leave a spare fish on the shore or toss a piece of bread over their left shoulder into the ocean.

Moryana is a sea spirit from Slavic folklore. She can change into a fish and likes to swim in the deep ocean with dolphins. She controls the winds and if she is angered, storms will blow.

Sedna, the Inuit spirit of the sea, lives at the very bottom of the ocean and keeps all sea creatures entangled in her long hair. Sedna only releases them when offerings are made or songs are sung in her honor.

16

In Greek mythology, the Nereids represent all that is good about the ocean. They often act as attendants to the sea god Poseidon and are said to rescue sailors in trouble.

In Polynesian mythology, Tahoratakarar was raised by the sea after his mother was taken away by evil spirits. The sea built him a boat, and when a sailor drowns, Tahoratakarar travels to them in his "Boat of the Dead" and takes their souls safely to the afterlife.

Vodyanoy is an Eastern European water spirit feared by sailors. It looks like an old man, wears a hat made of reeds, and is often accused of tipping up boats or tangling fishing nets.

SHAPE-SHIFTERS OF THE OCEANS

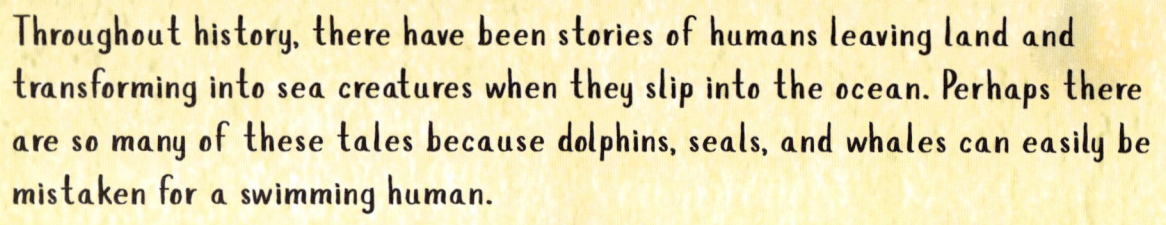

Throughout history, there have been stories of humans leaving land and transforming into sea creatures when they slip into the ocean. Perhaps there are so many of these tales because dolphins, seals, and whales can easily be mistaken for a swimming human.

In Greek mythology, Proteus is known as the "Old Man of the Sea." He was said to know everything: past, present, and future. If you can catch him, he'll tell you the future, but you'll have to find him first. He can transform into any sea creature he likes, so he's difficult to track down.

Akh'lut is a ferocious shapeshifter from Yupik folklore in the Bering Strait region of Alaska, USA. In the water, Akh'lut has the form of an enormous orca, but as it emerges from the seas, it changes into a giant wolf and walks on land.

Kushtaka can transform from human to sea otter. But be wary of these shapeshifters from Alaskan Tlingit culture. They use their cuteness to lure people into the ocean... and then steal their souls.

Hawaiian mythology tells of Nanaue, the son of a mortal and the King of the Sharks. He had a strange fish mouth on his back, and as he grew up, he began to shift into shark form in the water. Over time, he could no longer control his shark nature and was banished from the land.

In Europe, mermaids are traditionally half woman, half fish. If a human steals one of her belongings, such as her belt, comb, or mirror, the mermaid can become human and live on land. But if she finds her stolen object, she must go back to the ocean, never to return.

ARION AND THE DOLPHIN

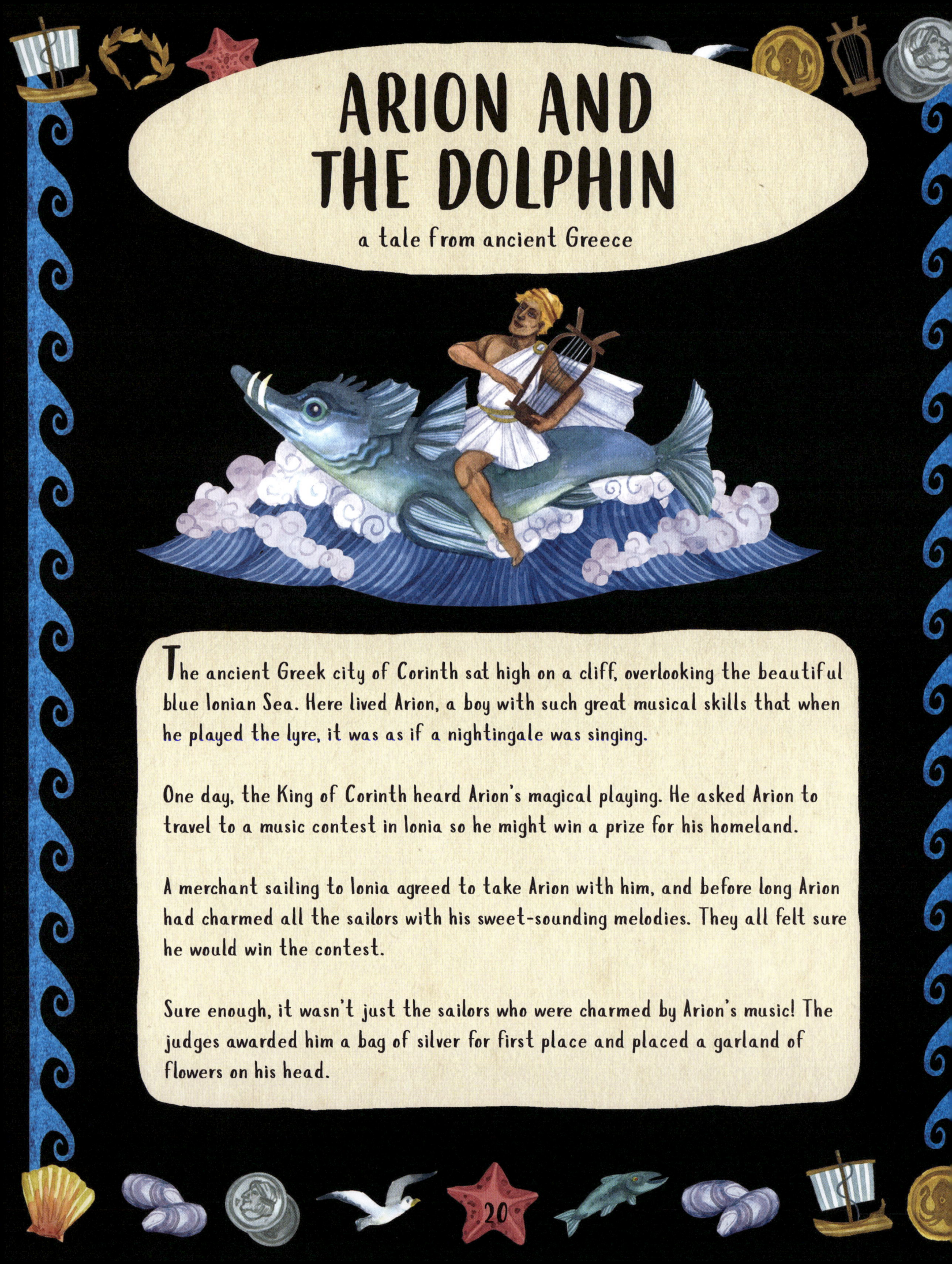

a tale from ancient Greece

The ancient Greek city of Corinth sat high on a cliff, overlooking the beautiful blue Ionian Sea. Here lived Arion, a boy with such great musical skills that when he played the lyre, it was as if a nightingale was singing.

One day, the King of Corinth heard Arion's magical playing. He asked Arion to travel to a music contest in Ionia so he might win a prize for his homeland.

A merchant sailing to Ionia agreed to take Arion with him, and before long Arion had charmed all the sailors with his sweet-sounding melodies. They all felt sure he would win the contest.

Sure enough, it wasn't just the sailors who were charmed by Arion's music! The judges awarded him a bag of silver for first place and placed a garland of flowers on his head.

Arion couldn't wait to get home to tell the king of his triumph, and so he hurried down to the port to find a ship. He thought luck was on his side when the very first captain he approached agreed to take him.

But after a couple of days at sea, the captain showed his true colors. He threatened to kill Arion if he did not hand over his bag of silver. Scared, Arion held back tears and begged to be allowed to play one last song.

The captain agreed and Arion stood on the ship's prow, playing a beautiful, haunting tune. As it drifted over the surrounding waters, fish, turtles, whales, and dolphins all rose out of the ocean to listen, and seabirds hovered over Arion's head, all enchanted by the song.

When he'd finished playing, Arion jumped into the ocean. He closed his eyes as he hit the water, expecting to sink forever into its depths. But instead, he felt himself rising out of the water... a dolphin had come to his rescue!

The kind-hearted dolphin let Arion ride on its back all the way home to Corinth as long as he continued to play his lyre the whole way.

The king's joy at Arion's return quickly turned to horror as he heard how he'd been treated by the sea captain. When the boat docked, the furious king went to meet the captain and asked about Arion.

"Oh, it was terrible," the captain lied. "A big wave came and washed him overboard!" The king stood aside, revealing Arion behind him.

The ship was searched and Arion's prize was discovered hidden in the captain's cabin. Falling to his knees, the captain begged for forgiveness.

Arion became a celebrated musician, but his favorite audience remained the sea creatures. Every evening, he'd go down to the seashore to play for the dolphins as thanks for saving his life.

WHALES, DOLPHINS, SHARKS, AND RAYS

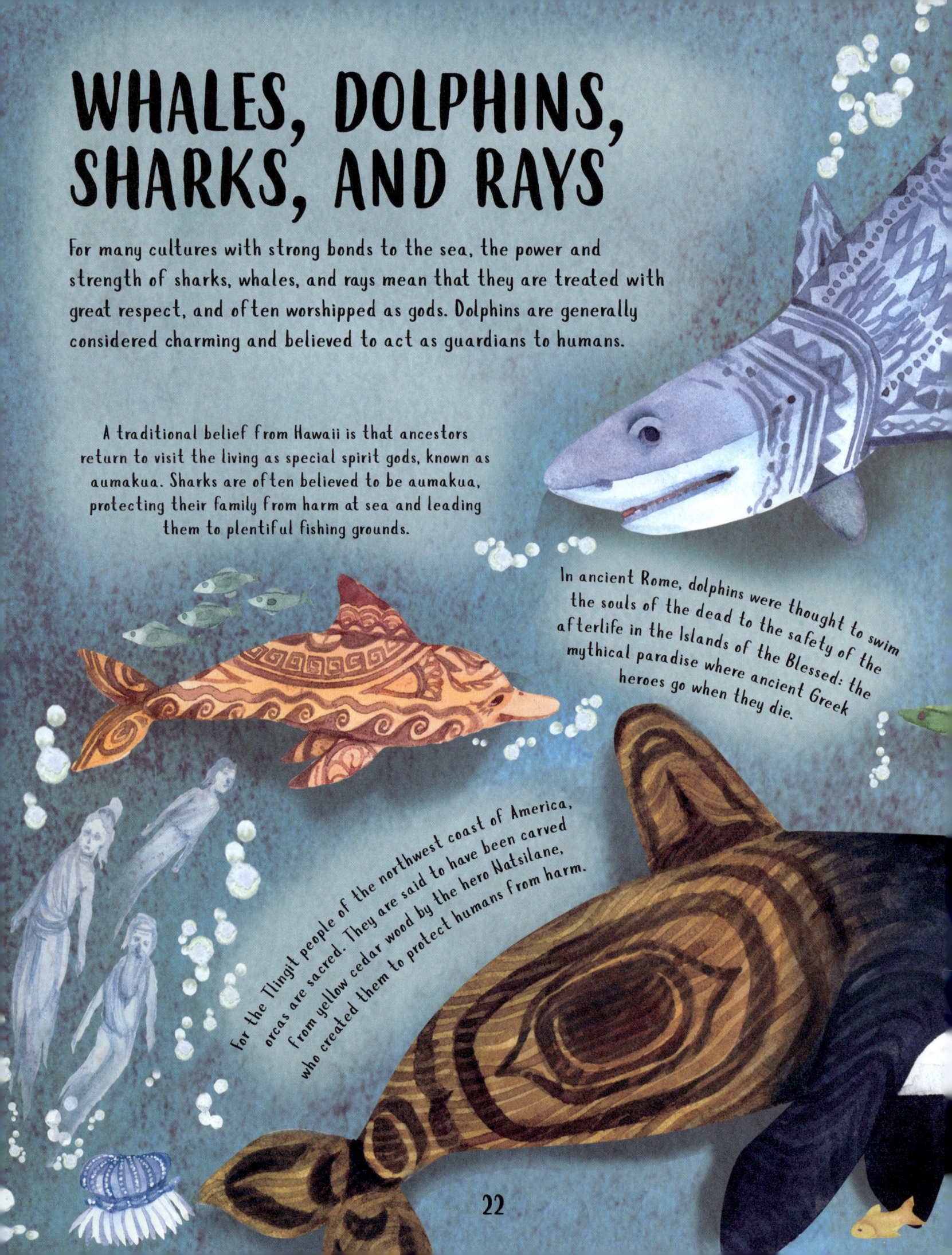

For many cultures with strong bonds to the sea, the power and strength of sharks, whales, and rays mean that they are treated with great respect, and often worshipped as gods. Dolphins are generally considered charming and believed to act as guardians to humans.

A traditional belief from Hawaii is that ancestors return to visit the living as special spirit gods, known as aumakua. Sharks are often believed to be aumakua, protecting their family from harm at sea and leading them to plentiful fishing grounds.

In ancient Rome, dolphins were thought to swim the souls of the dead to the safety of the afterlife in the Islands of the Blessed: the mythical paradise where ancient Greek heroes go when they die.

For the Tlingit people of the northwest coast of America, orcas are sacred. They are said to have been carved from yellow cedar wood by the hero Natsilane, who created them to protect humans from harm.

Whaitere is a stingray from Māori mythology who was carried by a wave into the Underworld below the sea by Hinemoana, the mother of the ocean. There Whaitere found her parents, who told her to return to the ocean and teach people to respect it.

In Iceland, some whales are considered evil, or "illhveli," and love nothing more than tipping over boats. To say the illhveli's name at sea is to summon them, so to stay hidden, sailors refer to whales using nicknames, such as "horse-whale" or "large-pig whale."

Kombumerri people from Australia's Gold Coast say that dolphins are ancestors of the white-haired dog trainer Gwondo. One day, children spotted a dolphin with a white fin in the ocean and believed it was Gwondo. It's said that Gwondo trained the other dolphins to round up fish, helping out the fisherfolk.

FISH AND SEA CREATURES

As thanks for the delicious and life-giving food the ocean provides, coastal-dwelling people often regard fish and marine creatures as gifts from the gods.

Haddock have dark spots above their gills, and in New England, USA, the marks are said to be the burning-hot fingerprints that the Devil left when he tried to catch the fish.

Indigenous peoples from the Pacific Northwest of North America tell of a god of the undersea named Kumugwe. He rules over the sea creatures and is responsible for the movement of tides. All the starfish in the sea are said to represent Kumugwe's great wealth.

Japanese Heikegani crabs have a pattern on their shell that looks like a samurai warrior's face. It's said that after the Heike samurai were defeated in battle, the crabs ate the warrior's bodies, absorbing their souls.

In South American Guarani lore, Japeusá was the third son of the first humans to be created. He was a trickster and always doing things backward to annoy and confuse people. When he died, he returned to life as a crab—and this is why people sometimes say that crabs are cursed to always walk backward.

An Estonian folk song tells that the small herring fish used to live on dry land and hated to get wet. It traveled in a boat full of salt but accidentally nibbled through the side. The boat sank, turning the sea salty, and from that day on herring had to live in water.

The Indigenous Inuit from North America say that salmon were created by the god Eqatlejoq, who whittled them from a walrus's tusk. As the tusk's flakes fell into the water, they transformed into scaly salmon.

25

SEALS AND TURTLES

Slow-moving and serene turtles are very ancient. As a result, they're usually thought to have played a role in the creation of the world. Seals are sometimes thought of as the dogs of the ocean due to their playful nature.

In the Orkney Islands of Scotland, it was believed that anyone who drowned in the ocean would return as a seal.

According to Hinduism, the whole world is balanced on the back of an enormous cosmic turtle named Kurma, who was a reincarnation of the Deva (god) Vishnu.

An Indigenous Makah story from the USA tells that two creators caught a thief. They decided to tie his legs together and shorten his arms into flippers, and this is how they created seals.

Chinese mythology tells that the creator goddess Nüwa cut the legs off a giant turtle named Ao and used them to prop up the sky after another god caused the heavens to fall. Thanks to Ao, the skies remain safely above our heads.

The minogame is a turtle from Japanese folklore said to live for up to 10,000 years. Over time, algae grows from its shell, dangling like an old man's long beard. Fittingly, minogame represent long life and wisdom.

In Scottish, Irish, and Icelandic traditions, seals are often thought to be able to transform into humans by taking off their skin. Selkies, as they are known in Scotland, can be summoned by shedding seven tears into the ocean.

Green sea turtles are seen as messengers between the land and the sea in Hawaiian tradition. Hawaiian sailors believe that turtles can help them navigate back to the shore, so they follow them.

SEABIRDS

On long sea journeys, miles from home and days from land, seabirds might be the only creatures that sailors see, aside from fish. This has led to all sorts of superstitions and beliefs linked to seabirds.

In Welsh tradition, Saint Cenydd was abandoned as a baby and cared for by a flock of seagulls. They carried him to the top of a cliff where they made him a bed from their feathers and protected him from the wind and rain with their wings.

The Celtic sea god Manannán mac Lir is known as the "son of the sea." He often takes the form of a seagull to fly across the water and act as protector to sailors.

The Polynesian Māori people call the rare Fiordland penguin Tāwhaki after the god who clothed himself in lightning. Why do these little birds have such a divine name? Because the crests of bright yellow feathers found over each eye look like lightning bolts.

The black guillemot is known in Iceland as teista, which means "the whistling bird." It was said that these birds would fly around the boat whistling to warn sailors that a dangerous whale was nearby.

When early European sailors explored the Southern Ocean, they came across colossal albatrosses: seabirds with the largest wingspan. They thought of them as bad omens, and seeing an albatross was said to be a warning of an approaching terrible storm.

The ancient Japanese tradition of fishing using cormorants is known as "ukai." The seabirds are tied to the boat, trained to dive down into the water to catch fish and return them to the fisherfolk. The fish are believed to taste much fresher when caught this way.

EERIE CREATURES OF THE DEEP

The dangers faced by those who make their living at sea have led to rumors of many menacing mythical creatures. They are said to lurk in the ocean depths, ready to tip over a boat or wash a sailor overboard. The vastness of the ocean encourages the idea that there might be creatures out there that scientists have yet to discover!

The yn beisht kione, meaning "beast with a black head," was a sea dragon imagined to live off the coast of the Isle of Man. Sailors hoping for a safe journey would throw a glass of rum overboard as an offering to the beast.

Chessie is a large sea serpent that's thought to live in the Chesapeake Bay in the mid-Atlantic US. Those who claim to have caught sight of it say the inky-black creature slithers through the waters like a snake.

The Bakekujira is a Japanese ghost whale in skeleton form. Coastal whaling communities were often thought to be haunted by the Bakekujira, who had absorbed the soul of a whale killed by hunters and seeks revenge.

The Lozi people of Zambia tell of evil sea snakes known as Ilomba. Witch doctors are said to make these fearsome snakes from their nail clippings. They then send them off to bite their enemies and steal their souls.

Lusca is a creature from Caribbean lore that is half octopus and half shark. It's rumored to live in blue holes, deep in the ocean, from where it attacks divers who dare to get too close.

SINBAD THE SAILOR AND THE ROC

an Arabian folktale

Sinbad was a fearless sailor who enjoyed nothing more than setting sail on great adventures. He never could stay on land for long before getting itchy feet. With the deep blue sea perfectly still and his ship full of goods to sell in distant lands, Sinbad set off on his second great adventure, sure that he'd soon make his fortune.

After a few weeks at sea, Sinbad and his crew caught sight of an island not found on any maps. Intrigued, Sinbad dropped anchor and went to explore. It was lovely to feel the sand beneath his feet, and soon he found a shady spot to take a nap.

When he awoke, he was shocked to see the sails of his ship on the distant horizon—his crew had sailed off without him!

Stranded, his dismay soon turned to fear as he spotted the mythical Roc flying high above him—a bird so large it was rumored to be able to carry an elephant.

The huge bird landed just a few feet from Sinbad, giving him an idea: what if he used the bird to leave the island? He untied his turban and used the fabric to strap himself to the bird's scaly leg. As the Roc took off, Sinbad watched the tiny island disappear from view.

They flew on for many miles before the great bird landed in a deep canyon. Sinbad climbed down and saw with amazement that the canyon floor was covered in glittering diamonds! But how could he scale the rocky cliffs and escape with some treasure?

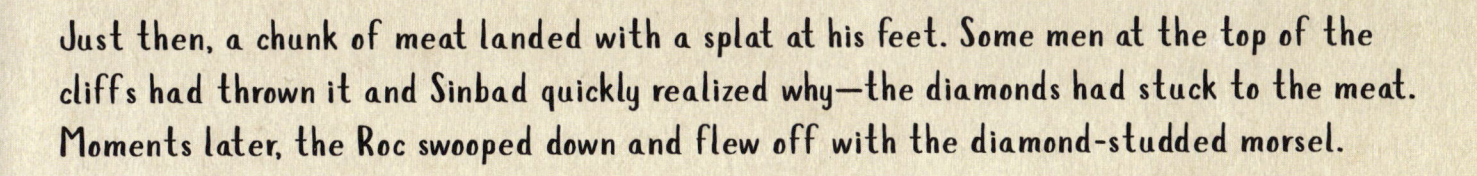

Just then, a chunk of meat landed with a splat at his feet. Some men at the top of the cliffs had thrown it and Sinbad quickly realized why—the diamonds had stuck to the meat. Moments later, the Roc swooped down and flew off with the diamond-studded morsel.

Clever Sinbad grabbed the next bit of meat and tied it to his back. His plan worked, and when the Roc returned to pick up the meat, he took Sinbad with it.

But he wasn't free yet. The Roc dropped Sinbad and the meat into its nest, filled with hungry chicks. Sinbad dived out of the way just in time as a razor-sharp beak lunged for the food.

A loud clanging noise suddenly filled the air, and to Sinbad's relief, the men who'd thrown the meat began clambering into the nest, banging on pans to scare the Roc away. Sinbad and the men filled their pockets with diamonds and quickly shimmied out of the nest. What an escape!

The diamond hunters welcomed a grateful Sinbad onto their ship and together they set sail. Once again, luck had been on Sinbad's side—and now he could start his next adventure!

SAILOR LORE

For thousands of years people have been braving the dangers of the open sea to explore, trade, and fish. Sailors from all over the world often work together on the same ship, and they have developed and shared many superstitions to bring them luck on their voyages.

Tattoos have long been popular among sailors, and the designs hold different meanings. A swallow tattoo shows that a sailor has traveled more than 5,000 nautical miles, as these birds are known to make long journeys but always return home, much like sailors.

Even today, the first time a sailor from the British, US, or Australian navy crosses the equator a "crossing the line" ceremony is held. A senior sailor dresses up as the sea god Neptune and welcomes the new sailors by dunking them in a barrel of salt water for luck.

Around the world, sailors agree that you should never sing or whistle into the wind on board a ship because it is thought to summon up a storm.

Sea shanties are a type of work song used to help keep rhythm while doing a repetitive job, such as hauling in rope. Sailors from all across the world worked on nineteenth-century merchant ships, and many popular shanties came from African-Caribbean sailors who often sang to keep time while rowing.

Ships commonly kept cats to control vermin, and the cats were closely watched as their behavior was believed to predict the weather. Licking their fur so it lay flat meant rain was approaching. Licking their fur until it stuck up meant a hail storm was coming. And if the cats were lively, then high winds were expected.

PIRATE LORE

Much of what we associate with pirates today—wooden legs, treasure maps, and parrots—comes from fictional pirates in famous books such as *Treasure Island* by Robert Louis Stevenson. However, there's lots of folklore out there that comes from real-life pirates.

It's said that pirates wore gold hoops in their ears to show they were "married" to the sea. Some sources say the gold was to pay for a funeral should they die at sea, while others claim pirates believed that wearing a gold earring improved their eyesight.

Blackbeard was a real-life pirate who wore flaming candles in his bushy beard to strike fear into his victims. They say that when he was caught, his head was cut off and his headless corpse swam three times around the ship before sinking.

Raising a black flag signaled that "quarter would be given," meaning that the pirates would attack a ship but not kill the sailors. A pirate ship showing a red flag was much feared because it meant "no quarter" and a bloody fight to the death.

Pirates would unfurl their flag to cause fear and warn nearby ships they were coming to plunder. The black flag with a skull and crossbones is known as the "Jolly Roger" and is the most well-known flag design, but some pirate flags were also decorated with hourglasses, daggers, and hearts.

During the eighteenth century, sailors believed that it was bad luck to have a woman on board a ship, so when Irish pirate Anne Bonny pillaged a ship, she would disguise herself as a man.

FISHING LORE

Catching lots of fish and avoiding rough seas are the main priorities for fishing communities around the world. To help reel in a plentiful catch, fisherfolk have developed lots of superstitions to bring them good luck.

In Brittany, France, the children of fisherfolk would sleep in a fish basket instead of a cradle. It was believed this would make them forever lucky at sea.

Fisherfolk in Ghana will not go fishing on a Tuesday because it's believed to be the day on which the sea needs to rest. Anyone fishing on this day is cursed by the sea gods.

Be careful what you say on board a ship. There are words that fisherfolk would never even whisper because they are thought to bring bad luck. Banned words include, "drowned," "good bye," and "good luck."

On the east coast of Scotland, fisherfolk used to collect a bottle of seawater on New Year's Day. The water was sprinkled around the house and seaweed placed around the fireplace to ensure a whole year of good fishing.

Hawaiian fisherfolk traditionally keep the first fish they catch and use it as an offering to the god of fishing, Ku-ula. They also take carved images of Ku-ula in their fishing canoes, as it is thought they will attract more fish this way.

The Indigenous Kwakwaka'wakw people of British Columbia in Canada wear salmon masks to dance and leap just as the salmon themselves do. This ceremony shows their deep respect for the fish and encourages the salmon spirits to bring more fish to the waters.

LEGENDARY VOYAGES

Stories about sailors who set off to explore the world have enchanted children for thousands of years. These exciting tales usually include impressive heroes, mythical creatures, and perilous journeys across the oceans...

The Argonauts were a group of fifty sailors who sailed with the Greek hero Jason to help him find the legendary Golden Fleece from a winged ram. Together they had many adventures, including outsmarting the Symplegades—moving cliffs that crashed together to crush ships.

Irish hero Bran went on an epic voyage that lasted hundreds of years. He was gone for so long that he was warned never to set foot on land again. When he neared Ireland, one of his crew jumped ashore and immediately turned to dust as the years caught up with him.

Sinbad the sailor is the hero from the Arabian tales One Thousand and One Nights who we met in the opening story of this chapter. He went on seven exciting sea voyages, including one where his ship stopped at an island only to find it was actually a sleeping whale.

Old Norse sagas tell of adventurer Gudrid Thorbjarnardóttir. She was one of the first to settle on the newly discovered island of Vinland (or North America as we know it today) more than 500 years before other Europeans began to colonize the continent.

In Vietnamese mythology, Lạc Long Quân was a great hero who set out to slay an evil monster that was terrorizing fisherfolk. He made a man out of red-hot iron and tricked the beast into eating it. As the monster choked on the burning metal, Lạc Long Quân cut it up into three pieces.

BOAT LORE

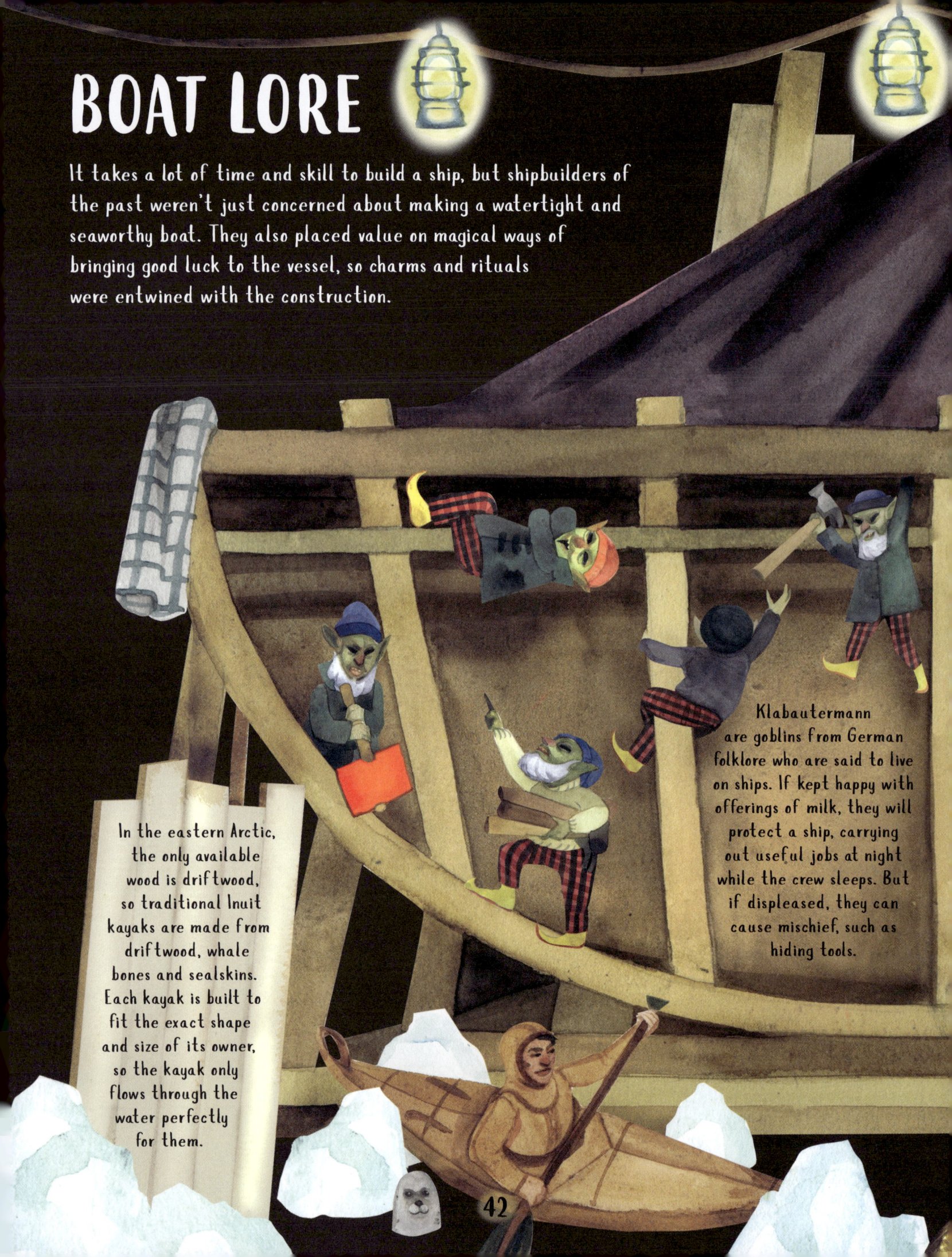

It takes a lot of time and skill to build a ship, but shipbuilders of the past weren't just concerned about making a watertight and seaworthy boat. They also placed value on magical ways of bringing good luck to the vessel, so charms and rituals were entwined with the construction.

In the eastern Arctic, the only available wood is driftwood, so traditional Inuit kayaks are made from driftwood, whale bones and sealskins. Each kayak is built to fit the exact shape and size of its owner, so the kayak only flows through the water perfectly for them.

Klabautermann are goblins from German folklore who are said to live on ships. If kept happy with offerings of milk, they will protect a ship, carrying out useful jobs at night while the crew sleeps. But if displeased, they can cause mischief, such as hiding tools.

When building a ship, it is considered good luck to place a coin underneath the mast. It's thought the tradition comes from the Romans who believed that when you died you needed to pay a coin to Charon, the boatman, to take your soul to the afterlife.

In China, large eyes were often painted on the front of a ship. It's thought that these would help the ship to "see" a clear route through the ocean.

For hundreds of years, seafaring civilizations have carved animals or people onto the prow of their ships. The Phoenicians, from the eastern Mediterranean, often had horses as figureheads to represent speed, while the Romans preferred wolves or boars, which were symbols of ferocity.

When building a traditional canoe on Taumako, in the Solomon Islands, the whole community helps out. The men carve the body of the canoe, and the women weave the sails from leaves. The sails represent Lata, their ancestor who was said to have made the first voyaging canoe.

A WHISPER IN THE WIND

an American tale

Skipper Perkins was a very successful fisherman with a whole fleet of boats, but he was mean and cranky. Each night he loved to sit in his big house overlooking the ocean, counting all the money he'd made.

One bright spring day when he was out strolling by the harbor, a wrinkled old woman named Betty Booker grabbed of his arm. "Good morning, Skipper," she said politely. "May I trouble you for a small bit of halibut to put in my cooking pot?"

Skipper Perkins looked Betty up and down, taking in her wild gray hair, piercing blue eyes, and tattered clothes, and he shook his head. "Why should I give you any of my fish?" he sneered, "I work hard for my catch."

"Sure you do, Skipper," she replied, "but I am old and hungry, and you wouldn't miss one small halibut. It doesn't hurt to be kind."

"Get away from me old woman, you'll get nothing from me without paying," spat the Skipper, and he stomped off.

The next day Skipper Perkins headed out with his fleet of fishing boats as usual, but as he sailed out of the harbor, he caught sight of Betty Booker standing on the shore, watching over his fleet and whispering into the wind.

What she said no one will ever know, but as those magical words whirled and tumbled through the air, they churned up winds, darkened the sea, and caused the skies to light up with violent flashes of lightning.

It was the worst fishing expedition Skipper Perkins had ever been on. The enchanted gale battered the ship endlessly, tossing it this way and that. The sails were ripped to shreds, and all on board felt so seasick they could barely stand.

To make things worse, not a single fish went near their nets. After three terrible days at sea, Skipper Perkins returned to land poorer than when he set out, for he still had to pay all his sailors for their efforts.

Although he'd lost a lot of money, Skipper Perkins learned a valuable lesson, and he returned a changed man. His mean and selfish ways had been soundly blown away by the magical storm.

After the storm, whenever he saw Betty Booker, or any other person in need, he freely gave them some of his spare catch. The more he gave, the better he felt, and the better he felt, the more fish he caught!

WAVES AND WHIRLPOOLS

Out at sea, churning whirlpools and rolling waves seem to appear from nowhere, and their great power can toss even the largest of ships from side to side with ease. Many myths and legends have sprung up to explain these sudden swells of water.

Tsunamis are enormous waves that are caused by earthquakes under the ocean. But according to Japanese mythology, the real culprit is a giant catfish called Namazu. It's said to live deep underground, causing tsunamis when it lashes its powerful tail.

When the woman Charybdis angered the Greek god Zeus, he turned her into a sea monster and chained her to the ocean floor as punishment. Charybdis was cursed to be terribly thirsty and so three times a day she sucks in huge mouthfuls of seawater, causing powerful whirlpools that sink any passing boat.

The Moken people from Thailand tell of the sea monster Laboon, who is sent by their ancestors to cleanse the world. Laboon spews seawater out of its giant mouth, causing an enormous destructive wave. The wave washes away anything bad and creates space for a better world to emerge.

In Norse mythology, sea gods Rán and Aegir have nine daughters, known as the "Billow Maidens," who can control the oceans. Their names each represent a different feature of the waves: Hefring for "rising wave," Kólga is "cold wave" and Bylgja means "rolling wave."

In between the Scottish islands of Jura and Scarba churns a huge whirlpool, known as the Corryvreckan. Legend has it that it was conjured by a sea witch to protect Scotland from a wicked pirate.

STORMS AND TYPHOONS

Sea storms usually seem to build up slowly with darkening skies and increasingly choppy waters. This is perhaps why many cultures have imagined that storms at sea are conjured up by an angry god, goddess, or spirit.

The word hurricane originally comes from the Taíno peoples of South America and the Caribbean. They used the word "hurakán" to describe the heavy storms that battered their lands, which they believed were caused by the angry wind goddess Guabancex.

Aegir was the Norse god of the oceans who ruled the waves. He was often depicted as an old man with long, white hair and beard who burst up out of the depths to cause shipwrecks.

Irish god of the dead, Donn, was associated with shipwrecks and sea storms. When a gale was brewing over the ocean, it was said that Donn was riding his white horse through the clouds.

The Hecatoncheires of Greek mythology were three giant brothers with fifty heads and a hundred hands. They were rewarded with palaces under the water after they helped Zeus defeat the Titans. At the bidding of the gods, they will cause violent sea storms with their many hands.

In Japanese mythology, Raijin, god of lightning, thunder, and storms sent the "divine wind," kamikaze, to stir up fierce typhoons to protect Japan from a fleet of invading Mongols.

The Blue Men of the Minch are sea spirits who live in the waters of the Outer Hebrides, islands off the west coast of Scotland. Some say that when they are asleep, the waters are still and safe, but when they are awoken, they use their great strength to stir up violent sea storms.

SEA WINDS AND MISTS

The powerful winds blowing across the ocean seem to control the coming of rain and storms, but they can also fill the sails of a ship to travel at speed. Folklore, myth, and legend provide many possible characters who might be responsible for controlling the sea winds.

Njord is a Norse sea god who could control the winds, waves, currents, and storms. He would help sailors in distress by calming the seas and creating favorable winds.

When the Milesians, the ancestors of modern Irish people, were invading Ireland, the old gods, the Tuatha Dé Danann, raised magical fairy mists to prevent them from landing. However, the druid Amairgen cast a spell to still the seas. The Milesians were able to land, and they defeated the Tuatha Dé Danann.

According to Philippine Visayan mythology, Saragangka Bagyo is a powerful and unpredictable storm god. One story tells how he transformed into an enormous bird and the flapping of his wings caused strong winds to whip up dangerous sea storms below.

Polynesian demi-god Maui was said to have captured all the winds, except the West Wind, and placed them in a cave bricked up with stones. Occasionally, he releases them to create a furious sea storm, which he rides in search of the West Wind, but it always eludes him.

In Hawaiian legend, Paka'a is a wind god who keeps all the winds inside the dried skin of a gourd fruit. He can release the winds by chanting their names, and he is said to have invented the sail in order to win a race.

SEA-WEATHER LORE

Sailors need to be very good at reading signs from nature, as they can warn of bad weather or rough seas ahead. Lots of the traditional weather lore used by English-speaking sailors has some basis in fact and is often given in simple rhymes so they are easy to remember.

Sailors say: "Red sky at night, sailor's delight; red sky in the morning, sailor's warning." And there's some truth to it. Red skies appear when dust is trapped in the atmosphere by high air pressure. High pressure in the evening usually means good weather is on the way, whereas in the morning it can mean the calm weather will soon end.

Sounds traveling through humid or wet air can become muffled, which has given rise to the saying: "When boat horns sound hollow, rain will surely follow."

A common sailor saying is "Mares' tails and mackerel scales make tall ships carry low sails." This refers to certain types of clouds, which can warn of incoming high winds. If sailors spotted these clouds, they'd lower the sails to protect them.

Some rhymes give advice on the best weather to set sail in: "When the wind is blowing in the North, no fisherman should set forth... When the wind is blowing in the West, that's when the fishing's best!"

Sailors watched seabirds for signs of bad weather, and the saying goes: "Seagull, seagull, sit on the sand. It's never good weather when you're on the land." In calm weather seagulls fish over the water, but during stormy weather, they shelter on the shore.

WHY THE SEA IS SALTY

an Ilocano Filipino tale

At the beginning of time, the giant Ang-ngalo shaped the world. He placed the Sun and Moon in the sky and arranged the stars in charming patterns.

Next, he scooped up earth with his great hands to create the mountains and carefully covered them in trees. Finally, he spat into tubes of bamboo, sealed them, and tossed them into the ocean. Inside grew the first man and woman who washed up on the shore of the Philippines islands and populated them.

Time passed, the islands flourished and Ang-ngalo kept himself busy creating new things. When the sun was especially hot, he liked to go wading through the cool ocean, which at that time contained no salt. His giant footprints created caves and caverns on the seafloor.

One day, as he strode through the refreshing waters, he noticed a beautiful woman in the distance, waving a black handkerchief.

As he got closer he realized she was a giant, just like him, and yet she was somehow different... Her eyes were jet black and her long dark hair swirled around her like hundreds of tiny tentacles, filling the air with darkness.

"I am Sipgnet, goddess of the night," she said. "I am tired of the darkness and wish to live in a palace of pure white. I've heard you are a great builder, so I called you here to make it for me."

Ang-ngalo loved to work and was only too happy to be given such a task. He immediately set off to search for some white stone. He looked all over the islands but none could be found.

Suddenly, he remembered the last time he'd seen something white as snow! In ten great strides he traveled hundreds of miles and reached the Kingdom of Salt, where he swiftly fashioned brick after brick of pure white salt.

Next, Ang-ngalo built a network of bamboo bridges to stretch across the water and employed hundreds of people to carry the bricks from the Kingdom of Salt to Sipgnet's home.

For many days and nights, the people marched endlessly over the bridges with their heavy burden of salt. Soon it disturbed the goddess, Ocean, waking her from her deep slumber. Enraged, she rose up in a series of waves, crashing against the bridges and destroying them.

Sipgnet cried out as she watched her dream of a beautiful white palace wash away—she would always be in the darkness now.

But Ang-ngalo could not help her, for he was too busy plucking every single person safely from the ocean and placing them carefully back on land. The salt could not be saved and it sank slowly into the water where it dissolved, causing the sea to become forever salty.

BEACHES AND DUNES

Where the land meets the sea, beaches are found—their soft sand constantly restored and renewed as the tide washes in and out. But as flat beaches give way to sandy hills, the calmness is left behind. The shifting nature of rolling sand dunes has given them a more dangerous reputation.

In Cornish folklore, Jan Tregeagle was a cruel man who returned as a ghost after he died. To keep him busy, he was given a series of impossible tasks, including removing all the sand from Berepper beach—a job that could never be completed, as each time the tide came in, the beach was covered in more sand.

Malaysian folklore tells that many years ago the Underwater Kingdom wanted to invade the Land Kingdom. To scare them off, the Land People placed fires all along Pantai Pasir Hitam beach, and the ash from these fires is why today the sand there is black.

It is said that among the Sigatoka sand dunes on the island of Fiji, there's a small valley known as "darkness" that contains a door to the Underworld. The dunes were created by the serpent god Degei when he sent a tidal wave that engulfed the land with sand.

The beaches of Japan's Iriomote Island have star-shaped sand. Legend says that the beach was created after the children of the North Star and the Southern Cross fell from the sky into the ocean and were washed up on the seashore.

In Breton folklore from northern France, fairies bewitched a group of fisherfolk, turning them into six black and six white cats. They forced them to dance endlessly under the stars. The only way they could return to human form was to weave the fairies a golden cloak from the sand on the beach.

SEA CAVES AND COVES

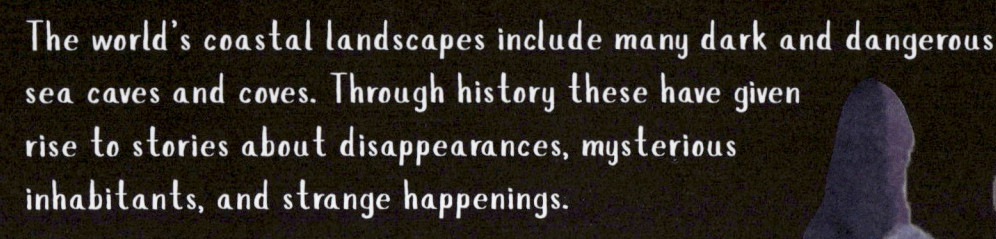

The world's coastal landscapes include many dark and dangerous sea caves and coves. Through history these have given rise to stories about disappearances, mysterious inhabitants, and strange happenings.

Sennen Cove near Land's End in Cornwall is said to be home to a magical mist. Whenever a storm is brewing, the thick white mist envelops the cove and a loud whooping noise booms out, warning fisherfolk not to set sail that day.

The Cave of Hercules near Tangier, Morocco, is said to be the place that the Roman hero Hercules rested before attempting to steal the Golden Apples from the Garden of the Hesperides. To make his way there, Hercules smashed through the Atlas Mountains, creating the Strait of Gibraltar between Europe and Africa.

The Japanese god of hunting, Hoori, fell in love with the sea dragon's daughter Toyotama. She became pregnant, but to give birth Toyotama had to return to dragon form. She asked Hoori to make her a nest so she could transform in private, but he peeked and she fled back to the ocean.

A myth about the Cove of Grennan, Scotland, tells of a piper who went to explore the caves that were rumored to be inhabited by fairies. The piper's music slowly got quieter as he ventured into the caves until it suddenly stopped. He was never seen again. Some say they hear the ghostly piping still.

A huge cave on the coast of the Hawaiian island of Kauai is known as the Maniniholo Dry Cave. It was said to have been dug out by the chief fisher of the Menehune, the mythical little people of Hawaii. He was apparently in search of an evil spirit who had been stealing all the island's fish.

COASTAL CLIFFS

Sea cliffs are land's dramatic ending before it gives way to the sea. Their craggy rocks, sheer drops, and crashing waves have inspired many myths and legends.

An Icelandic bishop, Gudmundur the Good, was asked to go and bless Drangey Island to get rid of a demon who lived there. But when Gudmundur met the creature it said, "Even evil must have a place to live," and so it was allowed to continue living on "Heathen Cliff."

In Irish mythology, a witch named Mal fell in love with the hero Cú Chulainn and chased him across Ireland. At the Cliffs of Moher, he leapt to an island but Mal followed, carried by the wind. He jumped back to the mainland, but when the witch tried to follow, the wind did not blow, and she was dashed on the cliffs.

An American tall tale tells of the great sea captain Stormalong, whose boat was so large he had to soap the sides so it could squeeze through the English Channel. As the ship inched through the water, the soap suds cleaned the rocks, creating the White Cliffs of Dover.

60

Spanish Cantabrian folklore tells of a wild girl who loved to go fishing on the dangerous Castro Urdiales cliffs. To keep her safe her mother cried out, "God grant that you become a fish!" and the girl was transformed into a mermaid to warn sailors to stay away from the cliffs with her song.

A South African Xhosa legend says the natural arch of the "Hole-in-the-Wall," found on the southeastern coast of the country, was formed by mythical sea people. They used an enormous fish to ram a hole in the cliffs after one of their kind fell in love with a mortal girl who lived on the other side of the rocks.

SUBMERGED CITIES, ISLANDS, AND CONTINENTS

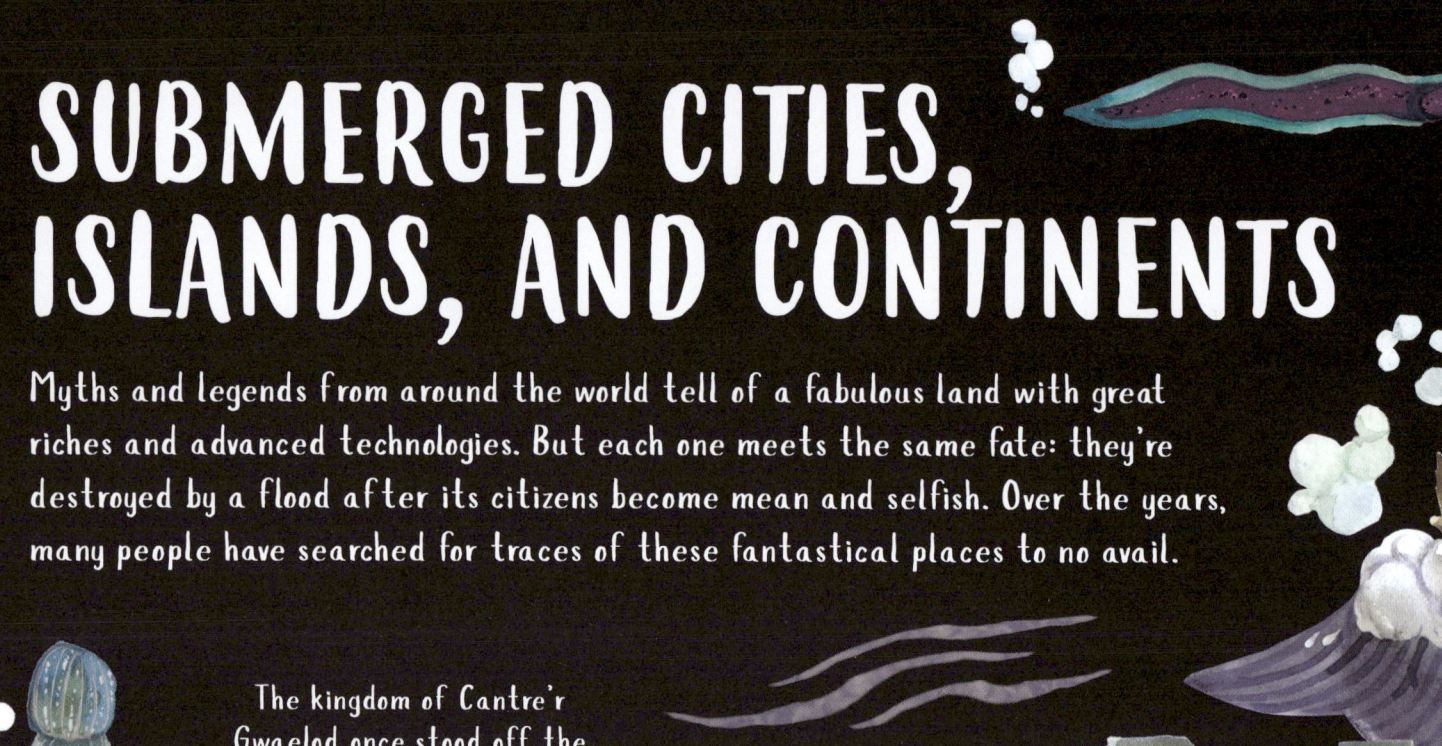

Myths and legends from around the world tell of a fabulous land with great riches and advanced technologies. But each one meets the same fate: they're destroyed by a flood after its citizens become mean and selfish. Over the years, many people have searched for traces of these fantastical places to no avail.

The kingdom of Cantre'r Gwaelod once stood off the coast of Wales in Cardigan Bay, protected by high seawalls. One night the guardian of the walls, Seithennyn, was so busy feasting in the castle that he forgot to shut the sea gates, and the whole kingdom sank beneath the waves.

Legend says that a long strip of land, known as Lyonesse, stood between the tip of England and the Isles of Scilly and was dotted with 140 churches. The whole area was flooded in a single night, but it's said that the church bells can still be heard softly tolling.

On the coast of southern India is the ancient city of Mahabalipuram. It's said to have had seven pagodas, but they were so beautiful that the god Indra became jealous and sent a flood to submerge them. Only one, the Shore Temple, escaped the flood and still stands today overlooking the ocean.

The Hopi people describe how their ancestors arrived in North America from the great continent of Kásskara, which sank, leaving just Hawaii and Easter Island still above water.

Kásskara

According to Greek philosopher Plato, the mythical island of Atlantis was a magnificent place with an advanced civilization who became greedy and immoral. The angry gods punished them with earthquakes, causing the whole island to sink into the ocean.

MYTHICAL ISLANDS

Explorers have long searched for mythical islands, rumored to exist in the world's vast oceans. They might have hoped to land on one of the wonderful places where life is heavenly, rather than the mysterious islands that are home to strange beasts and troubling spirits.

Hy-Brasil was a legendary island from Irish mythology where the High King of the World, Breasal, was said to have his court. Found in the western Atlantic Ocean, the island is shrouded in thick mist, only lifting and becoming visible every seven years.

In Slavic mythology, Buyan is an invisible island where a pure white stone called Alatyr is kept. The stone is the father of all stones on earth, the center of the universe, and has the power to grant eternal happiness. It's safely guarded by Gagana, a bird with copper claws and an iron beak.

Sixteenth-century sailors reported the existence of an "Isle of Demons" off the coast of Newfoundland in Canada. The mysterious isle was named due to the eerie wails and groans heard coming through the mist whenever a ship passed by.

Chinese mythology tells of floating mountain islands in the Gulf of Bohai where gods were thought to live. An elixir of immortality was hidden on the islands, and the First Emperor of Qin sent many men to try to locate the elixir and the gods, but they never succeeded.

Early Arab geographers described an island in the Indian Ocean known as Al-Waqwaq where only women lived. A tree on the island grew girls like fruit, and when fully grown, they fell from the tree making a "waq waq" sound.

Avalon was the mythical island off the coast of Britain where King Arthur was taken to be healed after he was mortally wounded in battle. It's said Arthur will return from Avalon in Britain's hour of need.

ASSIPATTLE AND THE STOOR WORM

a tale from the Orkney Islands

Lazy Assipattle did not enjoy hard work. While his brothers labored away cutting peat to use as fuel for the stove, he preferred to lounge by the family fire, imagining fantastic stories and dreaming of a better future.

You see, the kingdom where Assipattle lived was an unhappy one. For many years, a ferocious sea creature known as the Stoor Worm had terrorized his village.

Every Saturday at sunrise, the Stoor Worm rose out of the water to eat seven young girls. If the villagers failed to feed the beast, it would open its huge mouth, releasing a blast of poisonous breath, destroying everything in its path.

The king knew they could not keep the Stoor Worm at bay forever, so he asked the advice of his wisest wizard.

"Sire, the only way to get rid of the beast is to give it your only daughter," the wizard replied. "A princess will satisfy its hunger once and for all, and it'll leave these waters for good."

The king put his head in his hands. He could never sacrifice his only daughter!

There were just six days before the Stoor Worm returned, so the king sent messages across his kingdom begging brave young fighters to come and slay the beast.

Many heroes answered the call, but when most glimpsed the huge thorny head rising like a mountain from the water, they ran. The few who attempted an attack were soon brushed aside by the Stoor Worm's powerful tail. The king despaired.

Then, early one Saturday just before the sun rose, who should come forward but the lazy, good-for-nothing Assipattle. The unlikely hero had a plan…

Assipattle rowed his boat with its cargo of burning peat toward the worm's head. Suddenly, the Stoor Worm opened its mouth and yawned—Assipattle saw his chance. He pulled hard on his oars until his boat was sucked down the beast's throat.

The plan was working! Assipattle and his boat were washed all the way down to the creature's stomach. There he found the deep red mass of the worm's liver. Assipattle hacked at it with his knife, making a hole, then shoveled the burning peat inside.

The Stoor Worm began to choke on the billowing smoke and yowled as the burning peat seared its insides. As the worm coughed, Assipattle and his boat were expelled back out into the open water.

The king cried with joy as he watched the worm writhe in agony and die. His daughter and his kingdom were saved!

Within weeks, Assipattle and the princess had fallen in love and were married. No one ever called him a lazy good-for-nothing ever again.

GHOST SHIPS

You might think all ghost ships are alike, but you'd be mistaken. There are two kinds: the first are ships that were abandoned in mysterious circumstances and now sail the seas without a crew. The second are the stuff of legend—ships that haunt the coasts where they met disaster. Both types provide plenty of scope for storytellers...

The *Flying Dutchman* was a ship that was caught in a storm off the Cape of Good Hope in South Africa and went down with all hands on board. The phantom ship is said to reappear in bad weather and acts as an omen of disaster for any vessel that sights it.

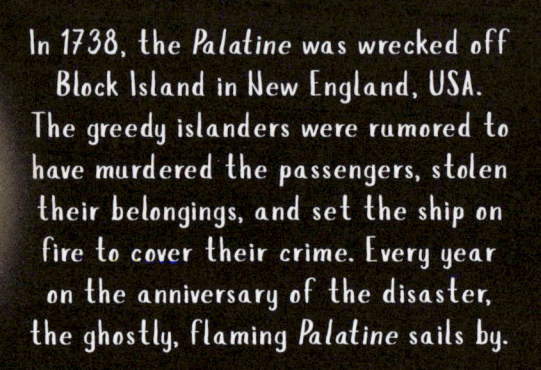

In 1738, the *Palatine* was wrecked off Block Island in New England, USA. The greedy islanders were rumored to have murdered the passengers, stolen their belongings, and set the ship on fire to cover their crime. Every year on the anniversary of the disaster, the ghostly, flaming *Palatine* sails by.

The sound of music and laughter can be heard before the magical *Caleuche* of Chilean Chilote mythology is glimpsed. Sailors who drown at sea are taken aboard the ghostly ship to join the never-ending party.

The Mary Celeste was discovered with not a soul on board off the Azores islands in the North Atlantic in 1872. The cargo was intact, the crew's belongings were in their cabins, and a lifeboat was missing. The crew were never found and many legends have sprung up to explain their fate.

Despite the superstition that it's bad luck to have women on a ship, the captain of the Lady Lovibond brought his wife aboard. A fight broke out among the angry crew and the ship was wrecked on Goodwin Sands, off the coast of Kent, UK. A ghostly version of the ship is said to reappear every fifty years.

The Canadian ship the Baychimo was trading furs with the Indigenous Inuit people in Alaska in 1931 when it became stuck in the ice, forcing the crew to abandon ship. A storm broke the empty ship loose, and it spent the next forty years gliding along the coast until it was presumed sunk.

MARITIME MISCHIEF-MAKERS

Many cultures have imagined evil or alluring spirits who try to tempt humans into the ocean. Some enchant their prey with song, while others resort to kidnapping, but all are dangerous.

The Sirens of Greek mythology lured sailors to their rocky island with a beautiful song. They were often shown as half bird, half human. The voyager Odysseus ordered his men to tie him to the mast of his ship so he could hear the song but would be stopped from jumping overboard to his doom.

Davy Jones's locker is the place at the bottom of the ocean where all drowned sailors are said to be trapped. Davy Jones himself is the sailors' version of the Devil, and he's sometimes said to be seen sitting in the rigging of a ship, waiting for fresh victims, just before a storm hits.

Adaro are Melanesian spirits from the Pacific Islands who are half fish, half human and have claws like crabs. They travel the oceans by rainbow or waterspout, and cause mischief by shooting people with flying fish.

In Japanese mythology, Funayūrei, or "boat spirits," are the ghosts of people who died at sea and have returned for revenge. They drown sailors and recruit them for their ghostly crew by using massive ladles to fill their boats with water until they sink!

Folklore from the Orkney Islands of Scotland warns of shapeshifting sea spirits known as finfolk, who yearn to kidnap humans and imprison them in their underwater palace. Finfolk love silver and the only way to escape them is by throwing silver coins in the opposite direction to distract them.

In Māori mythology, Taniwha are water spirits that often take the form of huge sharks or whales and act as protective guardians or dangerous predators to humans. One evil Taniwha was tamed by the hero Tāmure who clubbed the water spirit over the head, and now it eats crayfish instead of humans.

SEA MONSTERS AND SEA SERPENTS

Sightings of whales, sharks, and giant squid reminded sailors that the ocean is home to many dangerous and mysterious things. Glimpses of these huge sea creatures have inspired many legends of sea monsters whose only aim was to sink ships and devour their crews.

Leviathan, the many-headed sea monster from Hebrew scripture, was so enormous its size could not be comprehended by humans. When it rose out of the sea, fire blazed from its mouth, causing the water to boil.

The Dendan is a sea monster from Arabian mythology that can swallow a camel in just one mouthful and is said to be the biggest fish of all. However, sailors don't need to be afraid because if it eats a human or hears a human voice, it will die.

Resembling a gigantic octopus, the Kraken from Norse mythology was said to have tentacles that could reach for miles. It lurked deep in the North Atlantic Ocean, grabbing passing ships and dragging them under.

According to Filipino mythology, Bakunawa is an enormous sea serpent who lives deep in the ocean. Every now and then, Bakunawa catches sight of the beautiful full moon and emerges from the water to eat it, causing an eclipse.

Japanese Ainu mythology tells of the giant red octopus known as Akkorokamui that lived in Uchiura Bay in northwestern Japan. It's so enormous that when it rises from the water, the sea and sky turn deep red, warning the local fisherfolk not to head out in their boats.

PERILOUS STRETCHES OF WATER

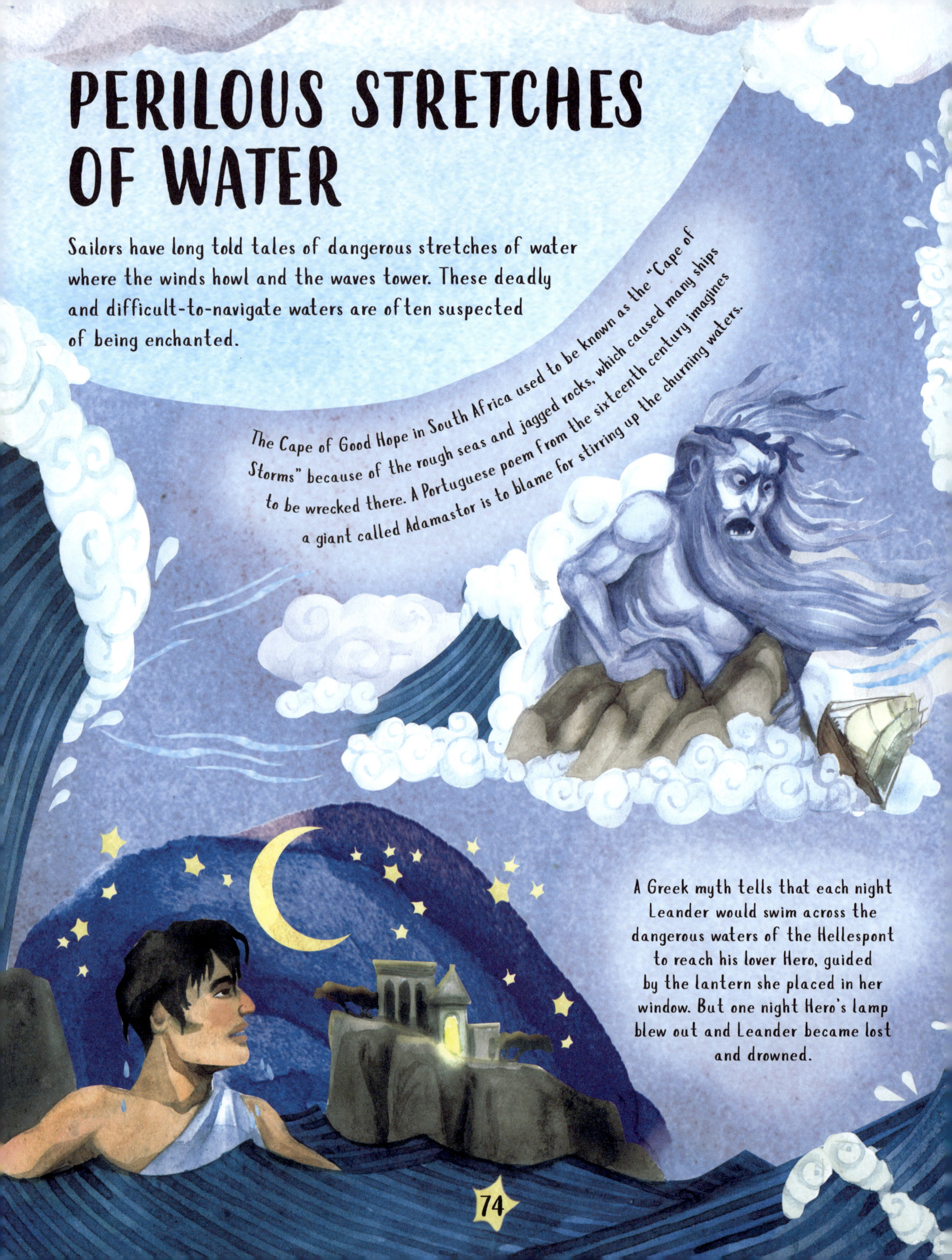

Sailors have long told tales of dangerous stretches of water where the winds howl and the waves tower. These deadly and difficult-to-navigate waters are often suspected of being enchanted.

The Cape of Good Hope in South Africa used to be known as the "Cape of Storms" because of the rough seas and jagged rocks, which caused many ships to be wrecked there. A Portuguese poem from the sixteenth century imagines a giant called Adamastor is to blame for stirring up the churning waters.

A Greek myth tells that each night Leander would swim across the dangerous waters of the Hellespont to reach his lover Hero, guided by the lantern she placed in her window. But one night Hero's lamp blew out and Leander became lost and drowned.

The Drake Passage is the spot just off South America where the Pacific, Atlantic, and Southern oceans meet. It's said to be one of the most dangerous stretches of water in the world. Sailors have nicknamed the voyage across it, where waves can reach 39 feet high, the "Drake Shake."

Aliens, underwater vortexes, and wormholes to another dimension have all been blamed for the mysterious disappearance of ships and airplanes in the infamous Bermuda Triangle, a section of ocean between Miami, Bermuda, and Puerto Rico in the North Atlantic Ocean.

When the legendary Māori hero Kupe first explored New Zealand, he sent his cormorant bird ahead to check the safety of the waters. The huge bird discovered the rushing torrent of Te Aumiti (French Pass) and drowned, his body forming a large reef which can be seen to this day.

GLOSSARY

Afterlife—the place where the spirits or souls of the dead are thought to go after death.

Celtic—the ancient culture of parts of Europe, including Scotland, Wales, Ireland, Cornwall, the Isle of Man, and Brittany.

Chaos—a state of complete confusion with no order.

Cove—a small sheltered bay.

Driftwood—pieces of wood that have fallen into the sea and, after being moved around by the tides, wash up on the shore.

Elixir—a magical potion.

Enchanted—placed under a spell.

Folklore—traditional beliefs and customs passed down in families and communities by word of mouth.

Folktale—traditional stories passed down by word of mouth.

Gale—a very strong wind.

Hurricane—a very powerful storm with strong winds.

Immortality—the ability to live forever.

Indigenous—the first people who lived in a land or region.

Mythology—traditional stories that are used to explain key issues, such as how the world was created.

Navigate—to find the way to a destination.

Omen—a sign or symbol that predicts something good or bad will happen.

Primordial—something that has existed since the very beginning of time.

Prow—the front part of a ship.

Sacred—something that is holy or connected with gods and goddesses.

Soul—the part of a person that, according to many religions, lives on after death.

Spirit—a supernatural being.

Tradition—the passing down of customs, knowledge, and beliefs from generation to generation.

Underworld—the supernatural world of the dead, often believed to be underground.

Witch doctor—a healer in traditional societies who uses herbs or spells to treat their patients.

INDEX

American folklore 24, 30, 44-45, 60, 68
Arabian folklore 32-33, 41, 72
Arctic 42
Arctic Ocean 10
Atlantic Ocean 10, 64, 69, 72, 75
Australia, beliefs from 23

Brazil, beliefs from 15

Canada 64, 69
Caribbean folklore 31, 48
Celtic mythology 28
Chile, beliefs from 68
Chinese mythology and traditions 15, 27, 65

dolphins 16, 18, 21, 22, 23

Eastern European folklore 17
Egyptian mythology 13
English folklore 16, 30, 56, 58, 62, 65, 69
Estonian folklore 25

Fijian folklore 56
Filipino folklore and mythology 54-55, 73
Finnish mythology 12, 14
French (Breton) folklore 38, 57

German folklore 42
Ghanaian folklore 38
ghosts 56, 68-69, 71
Greek mythology 11, 15, 17, 18, 20-21, 22, 40, 46, 49, 63, 70, 74
Guarani folklore 25

Hawaiian mythology 19, 22, 27, 39, 51, 59
Hebrew mythology 72

Hinduism 13, 26
Icelandic folklore 23, 27, 29, 60
India 63
Indian Ocean 10, 65
Indigenous North American mythology 18, 22, 24, 26, 39, 63
Inuit mythology and traditions 16, 25, 42
Ionian Sea 11, 20
Irish folklore 27, 40, 48, 50, 60, 64

Japanese folklore and mythology 8-9, 15, 24, 27, 29, 31, 46, 49, 57, 59, 71, 73

Malaysian folklore 56
Māori mythology 23, 28, 71, 75
Melanesian mythology 71
mermaids and mermen 16, 19, 61
Mesopotamian mythology 12

Norse mythology 47, 48, 50, 72
Norse sagas 41

Pacific Ocean 10, 11, 75
Papua New Guinea, beliefs from 13
Philippines, myths and folklore from the 51, 54-55
Phoenician traditions 43
pirates 36-37, 47
Polynesian mythology 17, 23, 28, 51
Portuguese folklore 74

rays 23
Roman myths and traditions 22, 43, 58

Sargasso Sea 10
Scottish folklore 26, 27, 39, 47, 49, 59, 66-67, 71
seabirds 21, 28-29, 53

seals 18, 26, 27
sharks 19, 22, 31, 71, 72
Shintoism 15
shipbuilding 42-43
Slavic folklore 16, 64
Solomon Islands 43
South Africa 68, 74
South Africa, folklore from 61
South America 25, 48, 75
Southern Ocean 10, 29, 75
Spain, beliefs from 61

Taíno mythology 48
Thailand, beliefs from 47
turtles 21, 26, 27

Vietnamese mythology 41

Welsh folklore 28, 62
whales 18, 21, 22, 23, 29, 31, 41, 71, 72

Yoruba mythology 14
Yupik folklore 18

Zambia, folklore from 31